PRACTICAL PUBLIC RELATIONS

Common-Sense Guidelines
for Business and Professional People

Sam Black

Melvin L. Sharpe

A SPECTRUM BOOK

PRENTICE-HALL, INC.   Englewood Cliffs, New Jersey 07632

Library of Congress Cataloging in Publication Data

Black, Sam,
    Practical public relations.

    "A Spectrum Book."
    Includes index.
    1. Public relations. I. Sharpe, Melvin L. II. Title.
HM263.B54 1983   659.2   82-21517
ISBN 0-13-693523-0 (pbk.)
ISBN 0-13-693531-1

ISBN 0-13-693523-0 {PBK.}

ISBN 0-13-693531-1

This book is available at a special discount when ordered in bulk quantities. For information, contact Prentice-Hall, Inc., General Publishing Division, Special Sales, Englewood Cliffs, N. J. 07632

10 9 8 7 6 5 4 3 2 1

Printed in the United States of America

Permission for printing the codes of professional standards, and information pertaining to objectives, membership, organization structure, services, and activities in the Appendixes has been granted by PRSA, IPRA, IPR, and CERP.

Manufacturing buyer Christine Johnston

Prentice-Hall International, Inc., *London*
Prentice-Hall of Australia Pty. Limited, *Sydney*
Prentice-Hall of Canada, Inc., *Toronto*
Prentice-Hall of India Private Limited, *New Delhi*
Prentice-Hall of Japan, Inc., *Tokyo*
Prentice-Hall of Southeast Asia Pte. Ltd., *Singapore*
Whitehall Books Limited, *Wellington, New Zealand*
Editora Prentice-Hall do Brasil Ltda., *Rio de Janeiro*

Contents

PUBLIC RELATIONS IN ACTION

Foreword

It isn't every day that an American author has the opportunity to provide input into the work of one of England's top public relations professionals. The result is perhaps one of the first efforts to provide an international approach to public relations practice.

As the American editor and contributor to Sam Black's work, I have attempted to expand the approaches to public relations provided by him. The result is the fusion of experience provided by the environments of two cultures, two different government structures, and two very different systems of public broadcasting. I have also attempted to update the changes that have occurred in the practice of public relations since the last revision in 1976.

We have much to give and share with each other on an international scale as the public relations profession comes into its own on a worldwide basis.

The late J. Carroll Bateman, 1980 president of the International Public Relations Association, referred frequently to public relations professionals as the "peacemakers" of world society. He appropriately did so in recognition of public relation's value and importance to world peace in facilitating communications and understanding between the governments and peoples of nations and between the governments and organizations and the publics that constitute nations. The late DeWitt C. Reddick, dean emeritus of journalism and communications at the University of Texas at Austin, called public relations the "lubricant which makes the segments of an order work together with the minimum friction and misunderstanding." It is hoped this book may help public relations professionals accomplish this goal.

Blessed are the peacemakers.

Melvin L. Sharpe

Preface

Since this book first appeared in 1962 there have been many changes in the world, but the theory and practice of public relations have not altered materially. There has been, however, a progressive acceptance of public relations in government, community, and industrial life.

Public relations interprets the present to the future and is an art applied to a science. The major new factor in public relations practice is the growing concern with the environment and with consumerism—the latter somewhat a reflection of the former.

Public relations can never be a substitute for efficiency and good policy, and one cannot overemphasize the importance of credibility. Once credibility is lost it is an uphill fight to regain the public confidence on which good public relations relies.

The structure of previous editions of the book has been retained, as it seems to have met the needs of readers of all kinds and particularly students.

Since the first edition was published, this book has been used by official bodies in the United Kingdom and many other countries as the recognized textbook for students studying for examinations in public relations. It is not possible for any one volume to encompass all that comes within the ambit of public relations, but the aim has been to give a good general survey of this interesting and fascinating subject.

I am once again pleased to acknowledge the advice and help of many colleagues and friends, and in particular the assistance of my late wife and partner, Muriel.

Sam Black

I

INTRODUCTION

1

Public Relations Today

The purpose of public relations practice is to establish a two-way communication to resolve conflicts of interest by seeking common ground or areas of mutual interest, and to establish understanding based on truth, knowledge, and full information.

The scale of activity to promote good public relations may vary considerably according to the size and nature of the interested parties, but the philosophy, the strategy, and the methods will be very similar whether the public relations program is designed to influence international understanding or to improve relations between a company and its customers, agents, and employees.

In a family or a small, closely knit community, there are few obstacles to mutual discussion and the communication of ideas, but even here there is plenty of opportunity for misunderstanding. In public or commercial life, however, the "family" circle is usually widely dispersed, and the absence of personal contacts makes cooperation and understanding difficult. People skilled in public relations practice use modern methods of communication and persuasion to bridge the gap and to establish mutual understanding.

DEFINITIONS

The difficulty the public relations profession has experienced in developing a definition acceptable to all practitioners is related to the complexity and diversity of the profession. The profession is comprised of many specialties using a diversity of specialized skills. These skills encompass professional knowledge ranging from that needed for entry-level and intermediate public relations and publication production positions to management consultation.

Simply defined, the term *public relations* refers to all the "publics," both internal and external, with which an organization has any contact and an organization's "relationships" with these publics. Relationships involve all forms of communication or the lack of communication. It must be remembered, however, that for communication to take place, there must be a give-and-take, or dialogue, between parties. Therefore, it is perhaps easier to develop a definition if we first examine the elements that must be present in a definition. Public relations is (1) a management function, (2) a communications function, (3) a research and evaluation function, and (4) a function designed to promote mutual understanding, harmony, and democratic input into the decision process.

Public relations is not a tool of business or of politicians, but it is a management tool. Nor is it a form of advertising or of journalism, although both advertising and journalism techniques are tools that may be used in public relations to promote communications.

Public Relations News has developed the following definition: "Public relations is the management function which evaluates public attitudes, identifies the policies and procedures of an individual or an organization with the public interest, and plans and executes a program of action to earn public understanding and acceptance."

The International Public Relations Association provides the following definition: "Public relations is a management function, of a continuing and planed character, through which public and private organizations and institutions seek to win and retain the understanding, sympathy, and support of those with whom they are or may be concerned —by evaluating public opinion about themselves, in order to correlate, as far as possible, their own policies and procedures, to achieve by planned and widespread information more productive cooperation and more efficient fulfillment of their common interests.

In 1948 the British Institute of Public Relations defined public relations practice as the deliberate, planned, and sustained effort to establish and maintain mutual understanding between an organization and its public.

Perhaps the part of this latter definition that requires most emphasis is the need for a public relations program to be deliberate, planned, and sustained. Relationships between individuals and between groups of people are fundamental and exist without any assistance from public relations practitioners. The function of public relations practitioners is to develop and encourage attitudes and behavior that will nurture mutual understanding.

"Practical" public relations is the professional attempt to achieve good public relations in order to promote the success or welfare of the company, organization, or individual on whose behalf the public relations effort is made.

The struggle for a simple definition of public relations that can be understood by the public as a whole and that will offset the negative use of the term as a description for "white wash" continues on the part of professional organizations.

The Public Relations Society of America established a task force to review the stature and status of public relations in the United States in 1980. Headed by Philip Lesly, the task force report cites two recommended definitions: "Public relations helps an organization and its publics adapt mutually to each other," and "Public relations is an organization's efforts to win the cooperation of groups of people."

A very sound short definition developed by co-author Sam Black is: "Public relations practice is the art and science of achieving harmony with the environment through mutual understanding based on truth and full information.

Whatever definition is eventually universally accepted by public relations professionals to describe their activities, the following principles and activities outlined by Dr. Melvin L. Sharpe in July 1982 and first printed in *PR Reporter* on August 16, 1982, Vol. 25 No. 32, must be recognized:

Public relations is the recognition and acceptance on the part of organizations of the following principles:

1. That the economic and social stability of an organization of any type is dependent upon the attitudes and opinions of the publics within its total operational environment.
2. That all men have the right to voice their opinions in relation to decisions which will directly affect them and, therefore, have the right to accurate information about pending decisions relating to them or their welfare.
3. That an organization's management of communications is essential to ensure accurate and adequate feedback from both internal and external publics in order to assure the organization's adjustment and adaptation to the change necessary for longevity.

The practice of public relations involves:

1. The constant evaluation and analysis of the operational environment of an organization and its publics.
2. The review and analysis of organizational goals, objectives, policies and procedures for the purpose of identifying lack of harmony between the organization and its publics or social environment and the potential short and long range effect.
3. The maintenance of open communications to assure the feedback neces-

sary for management decisions based on accurate and complete information and to assure the organization's ability to respond and adjust to change as required by societal and envirmonental conditions.
4. The planning and development of courses of action designed to project the organization honestly and accurately in order to earn and maintain the support and understanding of the publics within the operational environment of the organization.

Organizations which fail to accept these principles or which have communications programs which fail to perform the functions stated invite the problems that result from poor communication, resistance to change, management decisions based on inadequate data, and planning and programming which is stop-gap at best and minimal in terms of long range impact.

Although public relations principles and practice can certainly be applied and used by individuals, its professional context relates to groups of individuals with shared missions performing as profit, non-profit, political, or government organizations.

THEORY OF COMMUNICATION

Public relations philosophy puts much emphasis on the need for two-way communication. This is now fairly well accepted, but how does one achieve it?

Many forms of misunderstanding spring from lack of communication, and one of the first objectives in any public relations program is to improve existing channels of communication and to establish new ways of setting up a two-way flow of information and understanding. Even when there is a definite will to communicate, there may be great difficulty in achieving success, for the mechanisms of communication are very complicated.

Many of the difficulties in industry are ascribed to lack of communication, and managements are constantly exhorted to give information more readily and more regularly to employees and the public. Public relations methods can do much to achieve this, but let nobody underestimate the difficulties involved.

In a medium or large company there is a definite and closely related chain of communication from top management downward, and success in communicating clearly and quickly is essential to the efficiency of the company. Recent research has, however, revealed some discouraging facts about this important aspect of business.

It appears that a managing director should expect his deputy to understand only 60 percent of what he is trying to communicate to him on some important but complicated subject. In turn, the deputy will achieve only 60 percent understanding when he or she passes the information on to his deputy, and so on down the line of command. So if there are five levels in an organization, the junior manager may understand 13 percent of the original message. This relates to the spoken message, but the results from written communication may be even worse. The understanding of a written message may be as low as 15 percent at each level.

There was one encouraging feature of this research: When several different channels of communication are used together, the total result is much greater than the sum of the individual parts. This supports the findings of experienced public relations practitioners, who know that the best results in a public relations program usually come from tackling a particular problem in a number of different ways at the same time.

PUBLIC RELATIONS AND PROPAGANDA

A clear distinction must be drawn between public relations and propaganda. Goebbels described propaganda as "an instrument of politics, a power for social control. . . . The function of propaganda is not essentially to convert; rather its function is to attract followers and to keep them in line. . . . The task of propaganda, given suitable avenues, is to blanket every area of human activity so that the environment of the individual is changed to absorb the [Nazi] movement's world view." These quotations from Goebbels stress the great difference in the two approaches. Propaganda does not necessarily call for an ethical content, and the word is used these days mainly to describe those types of persuasion that are based solely on self-interest and in which it may be necessary to distort the facts or even to falsify them in order to achieve the purpose. Public relations, on the other hand, recognizes a long-term responsibility and seeks to persuade and to achieve mutual understanding by securing the willing acceptance of attitudes and ideas. It can succeed only when the basic policy is ethical and the means used are truthful. In public relations the ends can never justify the use of false, harmful, or questionable means.

It is not possible to use public relations techniques to bolster up a weak case; in fact, a successful public relations campaign may only expose the weakness. For this reason it is often stressed that good public relations must start at home. The policy should always be positive and constructive. Besides always being ethical, public relations must never be negative. Denials do not convince doubting listeners; a practical and positive demonstration of the facts is more likely to secure belief and constructive cooperation.

Under modern conditions, no government, industry, company, or organization of any kind can operate successfully without the cooperation of its publics. These publics may be both at home and overseas, but mutual understanding will be a potent factor for success in every case. Sometimes there will be overlapping; an employee may also be a stockholder and a customer.

Democracy cannot function properly without good public relations. Democracy has been defined as government of the people, by the people, for the people. The electorate requires knowledge on how government functions, information on decisions being made in its name, and education in order to take full advantage of the facilities and services provided. There is clearly need for public relations activities to help citizens understand their privileges and responsibilities under a democratic form of government.

The need is as great in local government as it is in central government, but while the obligation has been accepted generally by government departments and agencies in democratic countries, the same acceptance is not always found in local government.

Mutual understanding requires, by definition, a two-way communication. A public relations policy for an industrial company, for example, should include both inward activity and intelligence to assess the policies and behavior of the company to see whether action is necessary to improve the company's commercial image, and outward activity to inform the public about the company and its achievements.

Public opinion impinges on industry at many levels: with official bodies; contact with stockholders; relations with distributors, wholesalers, etc.; reactions of buyers or consumers; and internal relations with employees. In all these fields there is need for constant endeavor to establish and maintain mutual understanding and to keep a watch for possible causes of disharmony.

The social responsibility of industry is of prime importance to the welfare of a democratic society, and while many large companies have tackled this problem energetically, others have tried to pretend that they do not share a social responsibility and that they can adequately function in society without this recognition. History has repeatedly shown this assumption to be an incorrect one which, if not corrected, will be fatal to the existence of an organization.

DEFINING OBJECTIVES
AND PLANNING A PROGRAM

The methods and skills to develop mutual understanding can be provided by public relations activity, but first it is essential to define the objectives. Only when the objectives have been defined and agreed upon is it possible to plan the program. There may be both short-term and long-term objectives, and in both cases the timing is of prime importance. Some form of research will be necessary before any program can be planned completely, and it may be desirable to take steps to measure results as a campaign gathers momentum. The findings may indicate the advisability of amendment to the original plan, and it is wise to keep the campaign as flexible as possible to take into account any change of circumstances. Public relations practice is rather like playing a game of chess: 10 percent intuition, 25 percent experience, and 65 percent hard work.

A DUAL FUNCTION

Some of the confused ideas that exist about public relations spring from the fact that it is both an advisory and an executive function. Sometimes "public relations" is used to describe the advisory aspect, and "publicity" the actual execution of it. It is preferable to use "public relations" to describe the whole field, and it will be thus used in this book. Again, "publicity" is sometimes used to describe paid-for activities such as exhibitions, films, publications, etc., whle "public relations" is reserved for actions that do not direct expenditure. This distinction is quite artificial and of little practical value.

Public relations is everything from an attitude of mind down to a minute detail in the successful implementation of a program. As with many activities, it is possible to pick out individual acts for criticism or ridicule, but any serious assessment of public relations must take into account its full sphere.

There is an interesting analogy between medicine and public relations. A medical practitioner and a public relations practitioner must both first diagnose and then treat. It is common for both to be called in after the damage is done. Preventive public relations is just as important as preventive medicine and, like the latter, is equally inadequately employed.

CODES OF PROFESSIONAL CONDUCT

There are also points of similarity in training and professional behavior in medicine and public relations. After completing lengthy and comprehensive studies, a doctor qualifies by the passing of professional examinations and is admitted to the medical practice. A doctor may then practice as a general practitioner or take further training to specialize. Two common factors apply to all medical doctors: They all possess a minimum basic knowledge of medicine and surgery, and they subscribe to the Hippocratic oath.

A parallel exists for those engaged in public relations. All public relations practitioners—whatever their particular field of work—need to possess a basic knowledge and experience of the methods and media of the art and should subscribe to an accepted code of professional conduct.

The Public Relations Society of America has developed a Declaration of Principles and a Code of Professional Standards for the Practice of Public Relations. The International Public Relations Association also has adopted a code of professional conduct, and many national public relations associations have adopted their own codes or are considering doing so. Strict adherence to an appropriate code of professional conduct will do much to establish public relations as a profession and will help to maintain high standards. (See Appendix I for details of the PRSA Code, the United Kingdom's IPR Code, and the IPRA Code.)

The IPRA and the European Public Relations Confederation (CERP), at their meetings in Athens in May 1965, both adopted the International Public Relations Code of Ethics (see Appendix I). Codes of professional conduct govern the professional behavior of public relations practitioners in relation to people, and need therefore to be adapted to the laws, usages, and customs of each country. The Code of Ethics, on the other hand, sets out the moral considerations which must be observed by all in public relations in order to preserve the integrity of free communication between peoples and nations.

TRAINING AND QUALIFICATIONS

The progress made in the development of public relations education since Edward Bernays taught the first course in 1923 has been substantial. Compared to five accredited programs in public relations in 1966, twenty-five universities now have accredited programs. In addition, more faculty members than ever have backgrounds of substantial professional experience and an increasing number hold professional accreditation.

Instead of one course offering in public relations, accredited institutions are providing three or more public relations courses for undergraduate majors, and graduate programs are being strengthened with more than the one obligatory public relations seminar. Special courses in public relations are also being taught on many campuses in business, education, and government to improve the understanding of the importance of public relations to graduates of these disciplinary areas.

Many professionals are responding to the need for experienced professionals in the classroom and are teaching courses at nearby campuses in addition to carrying out their professional responsibilities.

The profession has also responded in providing internships for students and, to a more limited degree, fellowships and training experiences for faculty.

Research in the public relations area has increased, and the body of published material available on public relations is rapidly growing as evidenced by the Public Relations Society of America bibliography printed each year. Phil Lesly, Edward Bernays, Allen Center, Scott Cutlip, Alan Scott, Raymond Simon, and Douglas Ann Newsom are among the United States authors who have contributed substantially to the body of literature available.

Although substantial progress has been made in public relations education, the educational needs of the profession far outdistance the development to date.

The best evidence is the explosion of seminars and short courses constantly being offered to correct the deficiencies in education of previous years and to prepare current entrance-level professionals for their responsibilities. The cost to business for the remedial education programs combined with the cost of on-the-job training is staggering. The cost to the profession in terms of competence, efficiency, and reputation has also been high.

Professionals frequently express the need for graduates with a more thorough knowledge of government, of business terminology, of management principles, of research and survey technique, and with more highly developed writing skills and a more comprehensive understanding of design and what it can communicate. Above all, professionals want as entry-level employees college graduates who have been taught to think, who know logic, and who have developed a sense of sound judgment.

Students need a more thorough understanding of psychology so that they more fully understand motivation and persuasion; a better background in political science for the understanding of how government functions so that it can be made more responsive to societal needs; a complete understanding of anthropology so that they understand change and how it takes place and the importance of cultural adaptation; and of sociology so that they are able to more accurately evaluate societal trends and human interaction.

The interdisciplinary approach to public relations education is needed for greater progress in research as well as to provide a more complete and comprehensive education at both the undergraduate and graduate levels.

There is also a vital need for an identity apart from that of journalism, or of advertising, or of business, or of any other discipline. Public relations is too frequently viewed as a tool of business or of politicians, or as a form of advertising, or as a bastardization and somewhat tainted practice of journalism. If it is to be recognized as a science for the management of all communications for maximum feedback and input for mutual understanding, harmony, and democratic progress in society, then a distinctive identity as a disciplinary area without vested interest must be attained.

The establishment of independent departments or units of public relations in existing colleges or schools of communications is the most logical structure. Faculties of public relations could then be assembled which would include individuals with educational backgrounds in management, marketing, journalism, psychology, political science, anthropology, sociology, law, and public relations. The diversity of disciplinary background coupled with a core staff with ten or more years of practical public relations experience in the areas of corporate, counseling firm, and organization public relations would provide the student with an orientation not now available in public relations education and the profession.

The public relations profession will have reached maturity when accreditation is based first upon completion of an accredited degree program in public relations, followed by an internship period and formal examination.

Because of the wide range of career opportunities in public relations, the public relation profession's development will most likely parallel the medical and law professions with the educational development of general practitioners as well as specialists.

Educational programs in public relations are accredited today based on journalism curricula approved by the American Council on Education in Journalism and Mass Communications. It will be necessary, however, for accreditation to result from evaluation from a similar structure concerned specifically with public relations education before substantial improvement will take place in the accreditation process for public relations. Exceptions to this accreditation process are public relations programs located in colleges of business which are accredited by the American Assembly of Collegiate Schools of Business.

Public relations professionals with five or more years of professional experience may also seek accreditation from the Public Relations Society of America by successfully completing a comprehensive examination. However, it is becoming increasingly apparent that professional accreditation will not achieve the respect from members of the mass media press or of the public that a forthright policy of openness and full communication can achieve.

Today, entry into the public relations fields in the United States is best achieved following the completion of a degree program in journalism and public relations at either the bachelor or master's degree levels followed by internship or journalistic experience which develop writing skills and provide evidence of writing ability.

PUBLIC RELATIONS CONSULTANTS

It is regrettable that anyone can call himself or herself a public relations consultant—and many do—without possessing the requisite knowledge and experience. These untrained newcomers to the field tend to bring the practice of public relations into disrepute. A public relations consultant should be competent to advise a client on all aspects of the subject, and should be able to advise on the employment of experts when required for specialist subjects. A wide knowledge of the world is as essential as an understanding of public relations principles and practice. The practice of public relations consultancy is discussed in some detail in the next chapter.

The best criterion, at present, for a company or organization to use in selecting a consultant is to determine whether the consultant or consultants hold membership and accreditation in the Public Relations Society of America. But since educational standards have not been established, client relationships and records of performance are the only true indicators as to qualifications for consultancy.

A consultant in other professions is a highly qualified practitioner acknowledged to be competent to give expert advice, and this should apply equally in public relations. At the moment many so-called public relations consultants are competent only to provide a press relations service and are not qualified to provide a comprehensive public relations service.

A QUESTION OF STATUS
AND NOMENCLATURE

Public relations is an instrument of management, and public relations considerations should be taken into account when formulating policy, for public relations campaigns can never be a satisfactory substitute for correct policies. It has been said, with some truth, that public relations is 90 percent doing good and 10 percent talking about it.

In the United States the public relations chief sometimes enjoys vice-presidential status or its equivalent, but this is not the universal practice. The deciding factor ought to be whether the qualities of the person concerned qualify him for participation in top-management decisions in addition to his being responsible for coordinating and organizing public relations.

It is difficult to substitute a claim for the public relations head to be automatically a member of the top-management team; the level at which he works should be settled according to the merits of each case. Whatever the level, however, it is most desirable that he should have direct and easy access to top management and preferably to the chairman or chief executive.

The failure of some companies and organizations to establish public relations as an organized part of their activities may sometimes be due to the fact that the chief executive officer considers it to be his own personal responsibility to project the personality of the concern to the outside world. Many industrial leaders regard themselves as their company's chief public relations officer and react instinctively against any suggestion that this important function should be delegated to anyone, however skilled in the art of communication.

This attitude does recognize in part the importance of public relations. The chief executive officer should set the tone for the whole organization, but obviously he cannot spare the time to control the whole of the company's public relations activities even if he happens to possess the necessary ability and experience. In the same way that he relies on expert advice on accountancy, legal matters, architecture, sales management, etc., so does he need professional public relations advice and services.

The appropriate status that should be accorded to those engaged in public relations will depend on their responsibilities and to a certain extent on whether they are carrying out advisory or executive functions.

In a large industrial company control rests with the board of directors, and it is urged that the public relations advisers should be present at all board meetings so that they will be kept fully informed. The senior public relations executive should also receive all agenda and minutes and thus have the opportunity of raising any relevant matters in advance. The most important factor is for the public relations officer to be involved *before* decisions are reached instead of merely receiving instructions to carry out a decision.

The public relations staff needs to understand both the agreed policy and the reasons behind the decisions to follow particular lines of action if they are to be able to interpret policy intelligently.

The question of status links up to a certain extent with problems of nomenclature. Senior practitioners use varying titles, such as director of public relations, chief information officer, public relations adviser, information officer, director of public affairs, or publicity manager. A title sometimes bears a relationship to the responsiblities involved, but in most cases it will reflect organizational arrangements and does not indicate the exact nature of the work carried out.

MEASUREMENT OF RESULTS

Much of the doubt about the value of public relations arises from the difficulties in assessing the results of public relations activities and the absence of suitable yardsticks by which these results can be measured. Even where there are tangible results, as in press relations, the measurements can be misleading. Press clippings are a tangible sign of what has appeared in the press, but if the number of column inches is to mean anything, it is necessary to analyze these clippings according to type of journal, position in the journal, and also their content. It does not follow either that because something is printed that it is read, it is understood, or it is favorably accepted.

Furthermore, press relations are often valuable for their success in keeping the press informed and thus avoiding rumors or misstatements. These successes are certainly not measureable in column inches. This question reaches its acme of absurdity when sometimes press coverage is assessed at advertising rates and an attempt made to equate them to unpaid advertising. Press relations does not set itself out as, nor can it be, a substitute for advertising, for there is the great difference that advertising is under the full control of the advertiser, while press comment is susceptible to editorial rewriting, cutting, and even complete inversion.

Certain types of campaigns would appear to lend themselves to a degree of measurement of results. For instance, if public relations activities regarding road safety are stepped up during a period of several months, and the road casualty figures show a marked improvement in the same period, there is an assumption that the public relations campaign has been successful. There may, however, have been other factors playing an even greater part—weather conditions, for example.

This simple example emphasizes the difficulty of isolating the results of public relations activities. This is because public relations is an aid to management, a tool of democratic government, and a promoter of understanding at international, national, and local levels. It is rare that public relations can be isolated in its results; it is therefore, seldom capable of accurate measurement. It has been suggested that public relations performs a somewhat similar function to that of the conductor of a symphony orchestra in bringing out the best of the individual performers and in balancing their efforts. This is a useful analogy except that public relations, unlike the direction of the conductor, should be carried out unobtrusively as a part of established procedure for routine management.

FACING UP TO ETHICAL PROBLEMS

Most professional men are faced from time to time with situations that present ethical problems in which there is a conflict between personal gain and the ethics of their calling.

Mention has been made of codes of professional conduct, but ethics goes deeper than this. A code of conduct lays down rules for working with colleagues, relationships with journalists, and problems of this kind. More fundamental questions of ethics arise when considering such problems as whether a public relations practioner should engage his talents to promote something that he knows or believes to be evil, or contrary to the interests of his own country. These are deep waters, and the answer will often be a matter of conscience rather than logic.

The problem is likely to present itself in different form to those working on the staff and those engaged in consultancy practice. The ethical considerations are similar, but the practical manifestations are quite distinct.

It is to be hoped that any responsible person finds out the nature of the operations of an organization before accepting a staff position. If, however, it transpires at a later date that the policy of the organization is contrary to law or to his conscience, there can be no doubt that the public relations practitioner should resign immediately. This is an extreme example and one that does not arise often. It is more conceivable that there may be isolated actions that appear to be of somewhat doubtful honesty, or which may possibly conflict with the good of the nation or of individuals. In such circumstances it is essential and in the best interest of society to try to get these policies reversed, and if this proves unsuccessful then resignation must follow.

It takes courage to resign from a good position, especially if one has family responsibilities, but there can be no compromise with one's conscience under such circumstances.

To come down to more pedestrian considerations, it is very difficult to do good creative work under uncongenial conditions, and many public relations practitioners have given up comfortable and lucrative positions because they were not happy with their conditions of employment. Public relations is both a science and an art, and the best work is done by those working in a congenial atmosphere. Public relations work differs from that of, say, accountancy in that an efficient and convincing job cannot be done by an individual who has no faith in the organization for which he is working or in its product.

Ethical problems are likely to arise in a different form for those engaged in consultancy practice. Here it is likely to be a question of whether a consultant should accept a contract to promote a cause or product that might be considered undesirable by some people.

The PRSA and IPRA Codes of Professional Standards expressly forbid members to have anything to do with "front organizations." A member must not create or make use of any organization purporting to serve an announced cause but actually serving secret interests.

It is not necessary to be an ardent believer in a cause you are promoting, but it is unethical to work for a cause you believe to be wrong. For example, it would probably be generally accepted as unethical for a confirmed teetotaler to work for brewers or the wine and liquor industry.

It could perhaps be argued—to take another extreme example—that it would be wrong to do anything to publicize cigarettes, since smoking increases the likelihood of lung cancer; or to promote a wider use of butter, since it may be a contributory factor in the causation of coronary thrombosis. Like ethical problems in all other walks of life, those in public relations can present great difficulty at times, but they must be faced, considered, and dealt with according to conscience, for they do not lend themselves to solution by protocol.

Similar ethical problems are encountered in the political area. What public relation professionals must assure is that their own performance is above reproach and that their client or employer understands that compromise of ethical standards as described in the Code of Public Relations for the Practice of Public Relations or of accepted journalism, advertising, and broadcasting codes.

There is bound to be a measure of special pleading in all organized public relations activities, but it is a fundamental tenet of democracy that individuals and groups shall have freedom to persuade others, provided the means are fair and open. It is incumbent on all those in public relations, however, to maintain at all times a proper sense of responsibility, for their activities can influence the minds of men and have power over the progress of public affairs.

ADVERTISING AND PUBLIC RELATIONS

There is no general agreement as to the relative positions of advertising and public relations. As advertising is one of the means of communication with the public, a strong case can be argued for its inclusion as a part of public relations. The fact that advertising is paid for does not affect this general point. The image that the public has of a particular company undoubtedly derives in part from the type of advertising favored by that company.

This question is seldom faced squarely, and usually past precedent outweighs logic. The advertising department has deep roots, and since it spends a great deal of money, it often has a director responsible for its activities. Only in a few cases is there one man in charge of both public relations and advertising, although where this does apply it appears to work very satisfactorily.

In the future there is likely to be a swing toward this combination of the two functions, but it is likely to take a very long time to break down existing traditions. Where there are two separate departments in a company, it is essential that close liaison should exist, and it is helpful if both departments report to the same director or management committee.

An attempt is often made to distinguish between prestige or institutional advertising and advertising in support of sales activities. It is sometimes suggested that the former could come under the public relations department, but never the latter. This argument is not logical, for even in an advertisement offering some article for sale the face of the firm will emerge and make an impact on public opinion. For example, it is useless trying to promote the idea of a company being modern and up-to-date if the advertisements give a contrary impression.

LOOKING AHEAD

Public relations practice has become an essential part of modern life and has settled down to making an important contribution to government, industry, the community, and many other fields.

The efforts of professional public relations practitioners throughout the world to establish and maintain high standards of training and experience will bear fruit, and it will become difficult for individuals to claim proficiency in public relations practice unless they have had the requisite training and experience.

The moves toward the industrial integration of countries throughout the world have already had repercussions in allied fields and will undoubtedly lead to closer international links between those engaged in public relations.

SUMMARY

The ideas put forward in the preceding pages do not lend themselves easily to summary, but it may be helpful to list some of the things that public relations claims to be and the things that it is not.

What public relations practice includes:

1. Everything that is calculated to improve mutual understanding between an organization and all with whom it comes into contact, both within and outside the organization.
2. Advice on the presentation of the public image of an organization.
3. Action to discover and eliminate sources of misunderstanding.
4. **Action** to broaden the sphere of influence of an organization by appropriate publicity, advertising, exhibitions, films, etc.
5. Everything directed toward improving communication between people or organizations.

What public relations is not:

1. It is not a barrier between the truth and the public.
2. It is not propaganda to impose a point of view regardless of truth, ethics, and the public good.
3. It is not publicity aimed directly at achieving sales, although public relations activities can be very helpful to sales and marketing efforts.
4. It is not composed of stunts or gimmicks. These may be useful at times to put over ideas, but fail completely if used often or in isolation.
5. It is not unpaid advertising.
6. It is not merely press relations, although presswork is a very important part of most public relations programs.
7. Public relations in federal and local government is non-political. It is to promote democracy through full information and not to advance the policy of any political party.

2

The Practice
of Public Relations

The general theory of public relations leads logically to a discussion of the methods by which it is practiced.

OBJECTS AND AIMS

The practical applications of public relations practice can be summarized under three main headings:

Positive steps to achieve goodwill.   These consist of arousing and maintaining goodwill and public interest in the activities of an organization in order to facilitate the successful operation and expansion of those activities.

Action to safeguard reputation.   It is equally important to look inward at the organization and to eliminate customs and practices which, though legitimate, are likely to offend public opinion or to interfere with mutual understanding.

Internal relationships.   Using public relations techniques internally in order that the staff and employees of the organization shall be encouraged to identify their own interests with those of the management.

These are three main avenues of public relations practice, but there are numerous connecting alleyways which make it difficult to consider the three aspects quite separately.

It is the growing interdependence of industry at home and in the international field that has contributed mainly to the remarkable spread of public relations. This is shown strikingly by the rate of increase of the membership of the Public Relations Society of America and by the formation of national public relations bodies in practically all the larger countries of the world. PRSA was chartered in 1947 by a few enthusiasts, but by 1982 membership stood at over 10,500.

The practice of public relations has developed along two main lines. Many industrial companies, trade and professional associations, and federal, state, and local government agencies have set up public relations departments within their own organizations. Others have preferred to use the services of public relations consultants. Some use a combination of the two.

PRSA is a body of individuals and therefore includes in its membership men and women engaged in all types of public relations practice. The same applies to the Institute of Public Relations in the United Kingdom and to the International Public Relations Association.

Today there are ten professional interest sections within PRSA that provide members with the opportunity to participate in discussions and exchange views in these specialized areas of public relations practice: association, corporate, counselors, educational institutions, educators, financial institutions, government, health, investor relations, and utilities. Each section must achieve a membership of one hundred members before qualification as an official section.

THE CHOICE BETWEEN A STAFF OR CONSULTANCY SERVICE

It is often difficult to compare the relative merits of establishing an internal public relations organization or of using outside consultants, since there are so many varied factors involved. A discussion of these factors should help in the assessment of particular cases.

Some comments on consultancy practice have been made in Chapter 1. In general, the quality of public relations service depends on the ability and experience of those providing the service and not whether they are operating from within or outside the organization. When a consultant firm is employed it is necessary to examine the qualifications of the account executive actually handling the client's work as well as the expertise available within the firm.

Factors that Favor the Use of Consultants

1. The cost bears a direct relationship to the work commissioned, and the budget can be varied easily year by year.
2. The executives engaged on the account have worked on other types

of public relations for other clients and can thus bring their wide experience to the service of each client. Moreover, the combined experience of the staff can be brought to bear on very knotty problems.

3. The principles of the consultancy are independent and can thus give unbiased and impartial advice. Outside advice is often listened to much more attentively than equally good advice from one's own staff.

4. If the results are unsatisfactory it is an easy matter to terminate the contract by giving due notice.

Practical Disadvantages to Weigh Against These Points

1. An outside firm may have little practical knowledge of the organization's policy or day-to-day activities, and will require detailed briefing at the outset and at every new development.

2. There may be a lack of continuity in operations, for the personnel in consultancy firms are likely to change more frequently than those in staff appointments.

3. Queries from the press which are of any complexity will usually have to be referred to someone at the headquarters of the organization, and this hinders the provision of a speedy service to the press.

Factors that Favor the Setting Up of an Internal Public Relations Department

1. The staff become identified with the aims and objects of the organization and have a personal stake in its success.

2. They are able to assist the press without the constant need to refer to others.

3. Members of the staff are able to move freely within the organization and to establish friendly relations at all levels. This facilitates the promotion of internal public relations activities.

4. If the size of the organization warrants it, economy and efficiency can be increased by having specialist subsections to deal with the press, publications, films, photographs, etc.

The above considerations point out the answer. The desirability of establishing a public relations department or relying on the services of outside consultants will obviously depend on the size of the organization and the nature of the public relations activities it is proposed to undertake.

The carrying out of the advisory part of public relations would seem to be particularly appropriate to consultancy, but the exercise of the executive and continuing aspects of a campaign might be better covered by an internal staff department. An experienced public relations consultant is well qualified to advise an organization on the pros and cons of the adoption of a campaign or public relations programs, or to investigate and report on the effectiveness of existing activities in this field. Once the recommendations have been adopted, however, the most effective way of implementing the public relations program is likely to be the establishment of a public relations department or by the expansion of an existing department.

This may not apply in the case of small or medium-sized companies or organizations, where it may be uneconomical to make staff appointments and to run a separate department. A small organization may find it more satisfactory to use the services of consultants.

The above views are supported by the action of some leading consultants, who often recommend to large organizations which consult them that they should establish internal public relations departments, retaining their services in an advisory capacity. In some instances the consultant provides staff to form a department within the organization. They remain employees of the consultant and not of the organization for which they are working full-time. This may be satisfactory as a short-term measure but it is open to the criticism that the staff are likely to have divided loyalties and cannot identify themselves completely with the interests of the organization they serve. On the other hand, a public relations practitioner may sometimes have to give advice or take urgent action that is not particularly acceptable to the management, though it is in their best interests. At such times it is helpful if the practitioner's judgment is unfettered by anxiety about his personal future in the organization.

Even organizations with well-established and efficient public relations departments may find occasions when the service of consultants can be employed with advantage. This is likely to occur most frequently when onerous but short-term assignments have to be accomplished. It would be foolish to expand the size of the department to cope with transient difficulties, and it is much more sensible to use the assistance of consultants while the extreme pressure of work lasts. Another example might be when a specialist operation is to be undertaken that is outside the normal work of the department. One instance of this could be legislative or congressional lobbying activity, or, to take another extreme, the arranging of a press fashion show, which presents unusual difficulties. Because of the time involved in staff preparation, annual reports are frequently consigned to an outside firm.

A PARALLEL WITH THE LEGAL PROFESSION

Exact parallels from one field to another are difficult to find and may often be misleading, but a somewhat similar state of affairs exists in the manner in which organizations seek legal advice. A small company usually retains a firm of attorneys who will be called in to handle any legal matters requiring attention. A larger concern, however, will often have an attorney as a staff member to deal with legal problems that are likely to arise much more frequently. In such cases, an outside attorney will be called in for additional advice when necessary. There is a definite similarity here to the way in which public relations is developing.

ORGANIZATION OF A PUBLIC RELATIONS CONSULTANT PRACTICE

A factor common to all public relations consultants is that they are called in from outside the employing organization and have to justify their engagement by the work they carry out. This is both a strength and a weakness. It means that there is a constant need to make reports on work done, and a danger of favoring short-term spectacular projects against less dramatic long-term work that might be more beneficial to the client's interests. Not only does a consultant have to devote a considerable amount of staff time to making reports to existing clients, but there is also the need to contact and make proposals to potential clients.

Usually an organization first approaches a consultant with a view to engaging his services because of an introduction from a third party or through hearing about good work the consultant has carried out for another client. The organization obviously thinks that it needs public relations advice and services, and the first task of the consultant when he is called in is to prepare a proposal for the consideration of his new employer.

In most instances a considerable amount of work is necessary in order to prepare a detailed presentation on the public relations needs of an organization. It is first necessary to consider whether the particular problems are susceptible to treatment by public relations methods within the time available. It may require a considerable amount of research into the organization's methods and operation before a considered opinion can be formed. Frank discussion with the client is necessary, and there must be a clear understanding of the desired objectives.

The Budget

A consultant firm cannot provide a satisfactory service unless the client is prepared to pay an adequate fee. When a very low fee is quoted, it is foolish to expect very much in return. Most consultants consider that it is not possible to provide a comprehensive public relations service for less than two and one-half to three times the hourly salary cost of the employees to be involved, plus disbursements on photographs, entertainment, traveling, and so on. Employee salary cost is derived from the annual salary divided by 1,600 hours per year. These guidelines may not apply to short-term assignments or where a consultant is retained on an advisory basis. Such contracts would be budgeted in the light of the circumstances.

ORGANIZATION OF A STAFF PUBLIC RELATIONS DEPARTMENT

It is difficult to describe a "typical" internal public relations department, but there are many factors common to all regardless of the many differences in size and in the nature of the activities carried out. (Most of the following points apply equally to the internal management of a public relations firm.)

The first essential is good organization so that the best use is made of available staff and facilities. Full use should be made of modern equipment. The major cost in a public relations department is the staff and it is, therefore, desirable to do everything within reason to help the staff work efficiently.

Flexibility is another important point. It is impossible in a small office to split up the work into departments, and there should be as much doubling up as possible to ensure that important projects continue uninterrupted by illness or vacations.

The qualities that characterize success in public relations are discussed in another chapter; but reliability and flexibility are essential, and inefficient staff should not be tolerated since their failings can negate the work of the department. The tempo of work is usually fast and there is not time to check whether instructions have been carried out, so absolute reliability is very important. Moreover, unlike many other occupations, in public relations it is seldom possible to do one thing at a time, so a flexible, unflappable temperament is necessary.

The head of the department will inevitably impress his personality and his attitude to the work on those who collaborate with him, and since public relations is a very personal business it is unlikely that any two departments will be run in exactly the same way even in similar types of organization. The only criterion that can be applied in any case is whether the department works efficiently or not.

Many practitioners have had the challenging task of establishing a public relations department in an organization where nothing of the kind had existed previously. This provides an excellent opportunity to start in the right way, but the first task is often to educate others in the organization in order to make them understand the function of the public relations department and the manner in which it relates to other departments in the organization.

One danger is the tendency of top management to send to the

public relations department all queries and matters that do not fit easily into the program of other departments, or which appear to present little prospect of tangible results. The head of the department must be prepared to resist this atempt to make his department the repository of lost causes, and must be prepared if necessary to take his complaint to the executive head of the organization.

The point has been made above that the staff should be able to do many jobs, but nevertheless in a large department it is desirable to subdivide into several sections. Flexibility can be maintained by trying to see that staff do not stick in one section for too long at a time, but take a turn in each for periods of perhaps six months.

One subdivision will naturally be press relations. Other sections may deal with publications, including house journals and annual reports; publicity, including films, exhibitions, and displays; and a general section which will interest itself in such matters as the corporate image section which will interest itself in such matters as the corporate image of the firm, community relations, visits, intelligence, etc. Where the size of the operation warrants it, each subdivision should have its own head, each answerable to the head of the department who should take the closest interest in the work of each division without interfering unnecessarily with its day-to-day activities. It is a good plan to give colleagues a sense of responsibility by letting them sign their own correspondence and act on their own initiative as far as possible.

When an organization is housed under one roof, or at least in the same town, the public relations department is usually located at the headquarters. This is not an ideal arrangement, however, if the headquarters is in a remote area, especially for press relations. This is a problem to which there is no completely satisfactory answer. There is the further difficulty in deciding the best manner in which to organize public relations for a group of companies, or a single company with many branch locations. Probably the best solution is to have a headquarters for the public relations office and press office in a communications center for a state or region, with branch public relations offices in each branch location where large numbers of employees are located. However this problem is tackled, it will inevitably mean a great deal of traveling by the senior staff, with the attendant waste of time, but there is no way of avoiding it in these circumstances.

There is no necessity to fix an annual budget as there is when entering into a contract with outside consultants, but most large organizations cost every aspect of their operations and make an annual allotment to each department. Such a budget takes into account the staff salaries, rent, and other overheads and common services, in addition to actual disbursements. This gives a realistic picture of the cost of the public relations department. Sometimes a favorable comparison is made with the cost of using outside consultants by taking into account only actual disbursements and ignoring overheads. When a true comparison is made, the financial difference may be small. When there is only a small budget available for the public relations program, it is probably possible to secure more experienced services from a consultancy than by engaging full-time staff.

METHODS OF PUBLIC RELATIONS PRACTICE

The methods of carrying out a public relations program will be similar regardless of whether an organization uses the services of outside consultants, has its own internal department, or employs a combination of these two arrangements.

The media of public relations are the tools that are available to achieve the desired mutual understanding, and the various media of communications are described in detail in Part II of this book. These chapters set out the fundamental issues involved in the use of each medium, but many years of practice are necessary before anyone can claim a mastery of all these methods of mass communication.

The way in which public relations is practiced depends very much on the field of interest of the organization, although the basis principles are similar. In Part III, practice in a number of different fields is discussed in detail.

II

METHODS
OF PUBLIC RELATIONS

3

Press Relations

Press or media relations is probably the most important single part of public relations, but it is only a part, and it is important that this distinction should be understood. It is perhaps unfortunate that both public relations and press relations are often referred to as PR in Great Britain, as this leads to confusion. The problem is not common in the United States however, since the term media relations is more often used.

TWO-WAY COMMUNICATION

Press relations is essentially a two-way operation. It is the link between an organization and the press, radio, and television news. On the one hand, the organization supplies information and provides facilities to the press on request, and on the other it takes steps to initiate comment and news. Confidence and respect between an organization and the press are the necessary basis for good press relations.

Even in this radio and television age, public opinion is still molded mainly by what is read in the national, local, and trade press. It is essential to respect the integrity and traditional freedom of the press—a freedom that gives it so much of its significance—but it is nevertheless possible to seek the cooperation of the press for the furtherance of public relations objectives.

BASIS OF MEDIA RELATIONS

The best policy in media relations is to take the press into your confidence at all times. Tell the press as much as possible, even confidential matters, and then tell them which items must not be published and why.

It is wise to cultivate a balanced outlook toward press comment. The popular press will always prefer something sensational to news of steady progress, however important the latter may be to the national, regional, or local prosperity. There are, however, many opportunities for securing useful mention in the press if the needs of newspapers and periodicals are understood.

All newspapers are ready to publish hard news, even if their treatment of it may vary considerably according to editorial policy and the type of readership. A newsworthy story or item will always be welcomed by the press, and it is only necessary to ensure that the press receives the item expeditiously and accurately.

Today, however, a major part of press space is devoted to articles and features that give the background to the news, or to articles and features about matters of current or general interest. It is here that there exists an excellent opportunity of achieving the cooperation of the press in expressing the viewpoint and reasons for the viewpoint of special interest groups. Journalists require a continual supply of ideas and subjects on which to base their journalistic flow, and they are usually only too ready to listen to constructive suggestions. This situation might appear to open a door to undue influence, or even bribery, but it is rare for there to be any suggestion of corruption; indeed, undue hospitality often results in defeating its purpose.

A new professional respect is slowly developing between representatives of the press today and public relations practitioners. The press is beginning to recognize the value of having contacts within organizations which can provide information quickly and accurately. Competent public relations practitioners, in turn, respect the media representatives' role in providing balanced information to the public and understand the problems of expediency and limited space. Contributing to this professional relationship is the fact that many public relations professionals started their careers with news media experience, while others graduated from journalism programs in which they learned the concerns of the news media and the fundamentals of preparing media releases in acceptable style and format. Another factor may be the recognition by the press of the role of public relations practitioners in educating management as to the importance of honesty and full disclosure.

THE MEDIA RELATIONS OFFICER

It is often stated that media relations, press, or information officers hinder the press in securing news and stories, and that handouts have had a bad effect on standards of reporting. An officer's duty is to assist the press, and if he acts as a barrier he is failing in his job. For every press or news and information officer who hinders, there are hundreds who render invaluable service to the press by day *and* night. Handouts are a useful method of giving information to the press, but journalists should not use them verbatim—if they do so, the responsibility is theirs, and theirs alone.

A news and information office is not a policy-making body; it exists mainly to serve the press. The size and establishment should be related to the calls likely to be made on its services by the press, but it should be large enough to cope easily with normal requirements and to be able to overcome the occasional panic. It is essential for there to be arrangements for answering night inquiries for the benefit of the national dailies. Mention has already been made of the two prime considerations in media relations: speed and accuracy. If a reporter telephones with a query, he needs the answer quickly. If he cannot be given the answer, he should be told so and if possible referred to another source for the information he is seeking. If an editor asks for photographs, he should be told whether they are available or when they can be supplied. Whatever commitment is made for supplying information or photographs, it should be kept *to the minute*. It is exasperating for the press to have to telephone repeatedly to ask for the promised information. An incompetent procedure will quickly result in a lack of confidence.

The need for accuracy is obvious. Every step should be taken to avoid mistakes. Names or statistics given on the telephone may easily be misheard, for example. Some reporters will get the figures wrong regardless of the care exercised, but every effort should be taken to avoid contributing to the possibility.

Two very important factors in news media relations are timing and distribution: choosing the psychological moment to release news, and seeing that it reaches the right people.

Media relations is an exacting job if it is done with due care and conscientiousness. It is most undesirable for the press officer to undertake other major responsibilities in his organization, as they are bound to interfere with the efficient performance of his job as press officer.

The main justification for having a press officer is to ensure that the press can receive prompt attention to its needs. This purpose is negated if the press officer is so busy that he is seldom available to speak on the telephone. In too many cases it is more difficult to get the media relations officer on the telephone than it is to speak to the chief executive officer. This situation is more likely to arise when the head of the public relations department acts also as media relations officer.

Some press officers carry on happily in the belief that they are providing an excellent service to the press when they are not. A good way of checking effectiveness is to ask members of the press whether they are satisfied with the service they are receiving or whether they have recommendations for improvement. The results of such inquiries may be very revealing.

To establish satisfactory cooperation with members of the press it is necessary to understand how they work and how they think. It is not essential for a press officer to have been a journalist himself, but if he has not had personal experience of being a working journalist he should take the trouble to visit one or more newspaper offices and to study the conditions under which the press operates. It is essential to read regularly as many papers as possible, and it is also useful to try to write articles and features for the experience this will provide.

It is desirable to maintain regular contact with journalists by sending them background information, and not merely to approach them when some story has broken. It cannot be emphasized too strongly that the establishment of friendly relations with the media will yield good dividends.

It is also essential that an officer have a complete understanding of the goals and mission of the corporation or organization he represents so that a planned program of news releases and feature articles can be carried out which will convey and reinforce the message statements projected by the total public relations program of an institution. For example, if one of the message statements an organization wants to convey based on fact is research contribution, a press officer must be alert to the development of feature stories that will convey those contributions and continually evaluate results which will lend themselves to hard news coverage.

If the nature of the organization is such that it may possibly be involved in disasters or emergencies, it is essential to organize routine procedures to deal with such situations. The press should know the name of the person who will act as spokesman under such conditions and where to contact him. Journalists should be given factual information in emergencies as fully and as quickly as possible, as they are the direct link with the public.

PROVIDING AN INFORMATION SERVICE

In return for publishing news sent by the public relations department of an organization, the press will expect to be able to seek information from the organization about itself or its industry. In some instances this may be for background information, but in others it may lead to press publicity beneficial to the organization's interests. At times the press may seek information which the management of an organization would prefer not to have publicized. In such cases, complete disclosure is the only alternative. If the subject is a delicate one, journalists may agree not to pursue the issue if they are told the reasons frankly. Concealment, on the other hand, is likely to inflame their news sense and to make them keener than ever to pursue the scent.

In giving information to a journalist it is important to make it clear whether the information can be quoted as an official statement and attributed to a particular individual or to "a spokesman" of the organization. The journalist may be told, on the other hand, that he can use the information provided no source is quoted; or that the information is strictly confidential and nothing may appear in print. Journalists will normally respect confidences provided they understand the need for secrecy. The mutual confidence that exists between the news officer and the press representative will be the determining factor as to the success of such an approach. It must be remembered, however, that the news media are competitive businesses and anything released to the press is subject to release. If confidentiality is essential, then confidential it must remain until such time as the information can be released to the news media.

The organized "leak" has become quite a popular device, especially with governments. When the press publishes "leaked" information, it arouses public reaction—favorable or unfavorable. If the adverse reaction is strong, the government then denies the report. Such practices should not be recommended or condoned by public relations professionals, however, as they undermine the confidence of the public, raise serious ethical questions, and result in a loss of respect from the press.

If the officer is involved, a loss of credibility will result. The practice also exposes the organization to charges of favoritism in the release of information.

All newspapers and periodicals, however infrequently they are published, aim to publish stories and features that are not to be found in the pages of their competitors. The difficulty in securing scoops is one of the aspects of modern journalism that is often blamed on public relations. The reason lies rather in the increased complexity of life and, to a certain extent, on shorter working hours. These factors make it more difficult for journalists to meet the men and women who make news.

A problem arises when an organization is preparing facts or figures for issuing to the press to coincide with an event that will take place in the near future, and a journalist—by chance or deduction—hits on the story and telephones for confirmation. There are only two possible ways of answering the inquiry: the truth or a lie. It may be tempting to deny the whole story, but this approach would destroy the possibility of cooperation with this newspaper or journal in the future. It is essential, both on moral grounds and in the interests of expediency, to provide the information requested and to explain why the story was to have been issued on a particular occasion. A further problem now arises: As the story has been uncovered, should it be released generally to the press or should the journalist who hit on it be allowed to reap the benefits of his initiative and perspicacity? Except where questions of privilege may arise, it is wise to let that journalist have at least a good start before releasing the information. If it is not a matter affecting policy, it is desirable to let the journalist have his scoop unchallenged.

A somewhat similar question arises when a decision is made as to which journal's news should be issued on any particular subject. The so-called selective issuing of information to the press arouses indignation on the part of those journals not selected, and as a rule it is far wiser to make a general release to all newspapers and periodicals likely to be interested.

ORGANIZATION OF AN INFORMATION OFFICE

The size of a news office staff may be anything from one or two to twenty or more men and women; obviously, then, it is not possible to discuss here every kind of press office, since the form will depend on the type of organization to be served. There are many general observations that can be made usefully, leaving the reader to adapt the general principles to meet individual circumstances. In general, the following points apply equally to media relations carried out by a public relations agency.

In large organizations the media relations office will often be a subsection of the public relations department, with the media relations officer under the jurisdiction of the head of the department. In smaller setups, the chief public relations executive and the news officer will probably be the same person. The media relations officer will usually act as the spokesperson for the organization, but obviously he or she should take guidance on policy from he head of the public relations department, who in turn is answerable to management.

It is desirable that all press inquiries should be channeled through the media relations or press office, and that there should always be someone there competent to deal with anything that is likely to arise. It is relevant to note that this single-channel method of dealing with press inquiries came into being at the request of the newspaper people themselves and was not an invention of public relations.

Although the news officer should act as spokesperson for the organization on ordinary matters, it is much better for the chief executive to speak for the organization on matters of vital concern to the public or to the organization. It is creditable that so many top business people find the time to appear on radio and television and to take part in public affairs. This is public relations of the best kind, and it should be the constant effort of press officers to get their senior executives to accept their responsibilities in this respect.

The work of a press or media relations officer falls into three categories:

1. Issuing news and initiating articles, features, and reports.
2. Answering press inquiries and providing a comprehensive information service.
3. Monitoring the press, radio, and television, and evaluating the results; taking steps where appropriate to correct misstatements or to initiate counterpublicity.

ISSUING NEWS AND INFORMATION

It is the duty of the public relations staff to do everything possible to facilitate the flow of news from the organization. This may involve a considerable degree of educational work, for top management may take a great deal of convincing that it is desirable to keep the press fully informed.

Press offices usually work under pressure of day-to-day requirements, but it is essential to plan ahead since some operations will be likely to require detailed planning. The timing of important events is usually known in advance, and special steps should be taken well ahead. If necessary, help should be sought from outside sources to ensure that a special event will be dealt with adequately when the time comes. Some firms specialize in providing such short-term services.

The initiating of articles is a very useful means of bringing the organization and its activities to the notice of a wide public. All editors are interested to receive suggestions for articles, and if the idea appeals it will result in either a request for an article to be submitted or for facilities to be provided for a journalist to obtain information on which to base an article. This practice is growing in industry where it is often considered most useful for the technical staff of the organization to contribute papers to the appropriate technical journals. Some companies attach so much importance to this point that they have appointed technical journalists to their staff whose sole job is to encourage the writing of papers by senior staff and to arrange publication in suitable journals.

In many companies, it is the rule that all requests for articles from members of the company should be dealt with by the news officer. This is a perfectly reasonable internal arrangement, but if interpreted too rigidly it can lead to friction with the press. If an editor writes to the chief executive of a company, he will not take offense if he receives a polite letter from the media relations officer stating that the executive has asked him to deal with the matter. In some instances, however, the

editor receives a peremptory letter from the press or media relations officer demanding that all future letters of this kind should be sent to him
and that on no account should the chief executive or members of the
board be approached directly.

ISSUING NEWS RELEASES

The most usual way of issuing information to the press is by the writing
of a press or news release. This is then mailed or delivered to the various
newspapers and periodicals and to radio and television news offices. It
should also be communicated to the news agencies, who has direct tele-
type contact with the main newspaper offices in the country.

The news agencies will edit the release and will not send it out in
its entirety, so it is always worthwhile sending out the full release as
widely as possible even though some of the recipients will have received
it over the wire earlier.

It is essential to keep an up-to-date press list so that press releases
can be sent out without delay. Most organizations will need several
press lists—each appropriate to different types of release. Keeping
the press list up to date is a boring task and is often left to a junior
employee. This is a mistake, as it is essential to have an accurate list at
all times. It is usual to keep sets of envelopes already addressed so that
it is merely a question of selecting the right set of envelopes and inserting
the release. It is also usual to address the release to the news editor in the
case of metropolitan newspapers, but when it is for other papers it can
be sent to the editor. In some cases it may be desirable to send it to the
city editor, science editor, social editor, financial editor, etc.

Where a press office is responsible for a group of companies with
varied interests, the compilation of press lists may become very complex
and it may be necessary to have a large number of different lists for use
as appropriate. One solution to this problem is to use a mechanized or
computerized system whereby the addresses of journals and newspapers
can be selected within seconds.

The physical effort in sending out a release is quite substantial, and
there are a number of specialist agencies that will send out press releases
to order. In addition, there are agencies that specialize in the development
of mailing lists as well as services that provide up-to-date directories of
news media and journal addresses.

WRITING A NEWS RELEASE

In preparing a press release, it is well to remember that it will have to
compete for attention with a great quantity of similar communications

that editors receive daily. For this reason it is a good plan to have a printed heading that will identify the source of the press release. Such headings are often in color, and should be in the organization's house style if it has one. Otherwise, a distinctive but tasteful colored heading is likely to be most effective.

It must be remembered, however, that if news releases are poorly written and contain little news value on any type of regular basis, the distinctive heading and organization identification will also earmark the release for the editor's wastebasket.

The name and address of the sender should be clearly indicated, together with the name, telephone number, and extension of the person who can provide further information if it is required.

The date should be given on the release, and it is usual to mark it "immediate" or to state a release time. The word *hold* is necessary if it is a summary of a speech that is to be delivered after the release date. Release dates are respected by the press when it is in their own interest; when they are applied to comparatively unimportant news stories, some papers will ignore the story altogether as a gentle reproof and others will ignore the release date! It is thus far wiser to mark the release "immediate" and to send it out so that it reaches the press at the appropriate time.

When press releases are issued by a consultant on behalf of a client, this fact should be clearly indicated and the name and address of the client stated, together with information as to where further details can be sought.

The press release should be typed, double spaced, on one side of the sheet using generous margins.

The release should be headed with a slug or title that explains the subject. It is not necessary to think up a clever headline—leave this to the editor. Accepted news style should be followed.

There is no mystique about writing a press release; it is merely a communication and should be written in the way most likely to achieve the desired result. If it is badly done it will undoubtedly find its resting place in a waste-paper basket. It will find a similar resting place if there is no useful information or news in it. However much it is disguised, a "puff" will be recognized by the recipient, and not only will it be torn up but it is likely to prejudice the reaction to future releases from the same source.

The prime requirement of a press release is that it should make its meaning absolutely plain and be free from ambiguity. Many releases of a technical nature that are sent out are far from clear and require a telephone call to the sender to elucidate the details. When this happens, the media relations office often attributes the ambiguity to the technical staff who insisted on certain phrases. This may be true, but no news and infor-

cer should issue a release that he himself cannot understand, however much the technical staff insist.

Sometimes a press release must run to several pages to cover the subject, but whenever possible it should be kept to one or two pages—about 300–500 words in all. Other information relating to the release can be appended on separate sheets, and this is preferable to making the actual release too long.

A release that is suitable for general newspaper distribution is unlikely to be equally satisfactory for issue to technical journals, and it is often desirable to prepare two or more versions. It is also a good idea to prepare supplementary facts that can be given to members of the press who may request additional information. By this means the reports appearing in the press are likely to be more varied in nature.

If individuals are mentioned, give their full names and state any official positions held. Explain the purpose of any organization if it is not generally known. Give precise figures in preference to approximations whenever possible.

Sometimes photographs are sent with press releases. Since prints are expensive, it may be advisable to indicate that photographs are available on certain subjects rather than to enclose copies with each release. When photographs are used they should be of high quality. Captions should be attached to the photograph, but in a way that will not result in damage.

PRESS CONFERENCES AND RECEPTIONS

The holding of a press conference has become an accepted means of issuing information to the press, and it is very effective if used with discretion. Some organizations, however, never miss an excuse for calling a press conference or holding a reception for the press. This may be due to a chief executive's inflated concept of importance or to the insistence of public relations consultants who wish to show activity on behalf of their clients.

A press conference should never be called merely to hand out a document or information that could be issued equally well by a press release. The main justification for holding a press conference is that the subject is an important one likely to elicit plenty of questions from the journalists present. Press conferences are also an excellent method of imparting background information off the record when it would be inadvisable to send it out in print. Do not—as sometimes happens—forget to tell the press if the information given out is off the record.

The press welcomes invitations to cocktail receptions provided there is news to be obtained or an opportunity provided to talk informally with the chief executives of an organization. It is no longer true—if it ever was—that the press will go anywhere for a drink: Lavish hospitality is never an adequate substitute for news.

If it is necessary to hold a press conference at very short notice, news editors may be telephoned individually or the news agencies may be asked to announce the time and place in the material sent over the wire to newspapers.

An invitation to a press conference should normally be sent out a week in advance. It should state clearly the reason for holding it and, if possible, the names of the principal speakers. It is desirable to give sufficient details to make the editor feel the event is worth covering, but not to divulge so much of the story that it might be considered unnecessary to attend. Clear information as to the location, date, and time should be given, of course—it is remarkable how often one or other of these essential points is omitted.

If the conference is of general interest, it is impossible to select a time of day that will suit all the press. The morning newspapers are not keen on carrying a story that has already appeared the previous evening in the papers and on the radio or television news. If the subject is a technical one it is probably preferable to hold the conference in the morning, as this will give the dailies time to prepare a full report, and a short report in the evening newspapers will not worry them. It is unwise to hold a press conference later than 3 P.M unless it is intended mainly for the weekly trade and technical press. A knowledge of the deadlines of the media it is most desired to reach will aid in making a decision.

Choosing a suitable day is also very important. In some cases there is no choice possible, as the announcement has to be made on a certain day. Where there is latitude, however, care should be taken to avoid clashing with any other events that may keep the press away and may compete unfairly for prominence in the papers. Fridays, for example, are always bad days for major newspapers.

Special arrangements have to be made with monthly journals, since they often go to press several months ahead. This applies particularly to popular monthlies and women's journals.

Some editors reply to invitations to press conferences, others do not, so it is seldom possible to know the probable attendance. It is always better to have too many seats than not enough. If the conference is called for 10 A.M., keep in mind that television personnel may arrive early to set up equipment, so the room should always be ready in advance. It is usual to have one or more tables by the entrance at which the press sign in and receive handouts and photographs. If a large attendance is expected, there should be several members of staff dealing with the arrivals to avoid waiting in line. A personal welcome from the press officer or his assistants puts the journalists in a good humor from the outset.

There is no need for elaborate arrangements, but it is helpful if there is a raised dais for those on the press conference program. They should have their names indicated on cards in front of them, and the wording should be large enough to be read from the back of the hall. All members of the public relations staff on duty should wear badges with their names; this is an obvious point that is often overlooked.

The main factors to consider in the selection of facilities are adequate parking, accessibility for the movement of television equipment to the conference room as well as within it, adequate lighting, air conditioning, and electrical outlets. Accessibility to telephones and typewriters is also important. The walls behind the conference area should also be plain so that distracting objects are not photographically captured protruding from the heads of participants.

When press conferences are held with some regularity, it is desirable for a soft blue curtain backdrop to be constructed and additional lighting to be installed.

The public relations executive who is in charge of the conference will usually welcome the media representatives and introduce the chief executive. The success of the conference will depend to a great extent on the speaking ability of the chief executive officer and others supporting him. If the chief executive is a poor speaker it is difficult to surmount this obstacle completely; the only hope is to try to persuade him to give a short introduction and to ask others to elaborate the various points.

The preparation made for a press conference is probably the most important factor in hosting a successful press conference. There are a number of training programs for chief executives which will aid them in fielding questions and prevent them from making misstatements. The training programs are sound and worth consideration.

However, the internal public relations staff can overcome many obstacles and prepare officials for the conference themselves with careful planning.

If a sensitive statement or information is to be presented where absolute accuracy is of most importance, then the first step is the preparation of the material, in which every effort is made to achieve clarity and to prevent ambiguity. Officers should then read the statements at the press conference and avoid ad lib remarks, which may result in unexpected confusion. Copies of the statements should always be available to the press along with background information when appropriate. Although it is preferable to provide handouts at the conclusion of the conference, reporters will normally want copies of speeches or statements to be made in advance so they can make marginal notations as they hear the comments.

Upon conclusion of the opening statements, the chief executive officer or the public relations executive will announce the entertainment of questions.

The best way to prepare executive officers to field questions is to attempt to anticipate all the questions that might be asked. The questions can be placed in a press conference briefing manual along with the carefully researched answers. The chief executive should then review the questions and answers until he feels confident in his knowledge of the material. The reason this procedure is important in a large organization or corporation is that no chief executive can pull all the facts and figures about his organization out of his head on the spur of the moment because of the complexity of the organization and the amount of detailed information one would have to know.

If the chief executive is unaccustomed to hosting press conferences, then a dry run can be held with public relations staff members and others firing questions to the chief executive until he and his staff feel comfortable with the responses and the manner in which they are delivered.

Should questions be asked at the conference that the chief executive or other officers present can not answer, the chief executive should simply state that he or she will have to look into the matter or acquire details and data and get back to the reporter who requested the information.

The public relations staff should always record the press conference so that comments can be clarified with the release of additional information, if necessary, and so that slipups do not occur in failing to provide reporters with requested information or assistance.

The conference should start on time and formal comments should be kept as brief as possible, allowing maximum time for questions. If there are few questions, it will usually indicate that the information presented was clear and complete.

Light refreshments are normally provided; they need not include alcoholic beverages. In some cases, a lunch is provided. The invitation should indicate clearly the nature of hospitality if anything more than soft drinks or coffee is to be provided.

If photographs are available, they should be given out in protected envelopes unless all the press information is handed out in a specially designed folder, usually referred to as a press kit. The number of materials to be distributed will determine the need for the press kit, which is simply a means of packaging the materials for the convenience of the press.

Follow-up steps should be taken to send copies of all the materials to the invited news media that were not represented at the conference.

Most of the above comments apply also to press receptions, except that the proceedings are much less formal and usually take place in the evening.

There is a growing tendency to invite many outsiders to press conferences and receptions—outsiders, that is, in the sense that they are not press. This is not to be encouraged, as it tends to interfere with the primary purpose of the function and is often resented by the press representatives.

FACILITY VISITS

It is human to be impressed more by what one sees than by what one hears, and for this reason visits to new facilities or production areas have an important part to play in public relations. Such visits fall into three main categories: visits by buyers or important business contacts; open houses for the public; and press tours.

There is no need to discuss the first group, and visits by the public will be dealt with in greater detail later. The question of press visitation, however, is both an interesting and a complex one.

It is common practice to issue individual invitations to editors or journalists, or to invite small groups of the press; but when a major event takes place, such as when a new factory is opened or a new power station commissioned, it is often the practice to issue invitations to the national, state, local, trade, and technical press, and to the radio and television media. The invitation list will naturally depend on the object of the exercise and what it is hoped to achieve. Whatever media are chosen, it is desirable to ensure that invitations are sent to all the press in that category.

Facility visits are both an excellent method of securing the interest and cooperation of the press and a very effective means of antagonizing them if the arrangements are poorly planned and executed or if they go away feeling their journey was not really necessary.

A visit to a manufacturer's works or demonstration often involves a whole day away from the office, with possibly an early start and a late return home. It is essential that there should be sufficient advantage to gain from the visit to compensate for this effort. An abundance of liquor and an excellent lunch will not be regarded as an adequate return by the press unless they are able to see something new or worthwhile on the visit.

A facility visit begins when the invitations are sent out; these should state clearly the nature of the visit and give all essential data. As much detail as possible should be given about transportation, meeting points, parking, hotels, expected time of return to starting point, etc. It is also important to state clearly on the invitation or the accompanying letter whether the sponsors of the visit are providing free transportation, hotel accommodation, or meals.

It is not essential to provide free travel, but it has become usual for this to be done on industrial visits. Government agencies are rarely able to offer free travel or hospitality. The essential point is to make the position clear on this matter, as it may in some instances influence the editor's decision to send a representative or not. Having to pay the expenses will not prevent a large attendance if the story is likely to be a good one. On one occasion, a trade association took a party of about twenty technical editors to visit an exhibition in another country. The association made all the arrangements for air travel, hotel accommodation, etc., and made an inclusive charge. The charge did not prevent a very high acceptance rate of those invited.

The invitation should indicate the latest date replies can be received, and it is helpful if a stamped, addressed card or envelope is enclosed. When acceptances have been received, it is desirable that they should be acknowledged and information given as to when further details will be sent to those taking part in the visit.

In certain circumstances there may be a choice of type of travel that can be arranged. If time permits, it is a good idea to ask those invited to state their preference so that arrangements may be made in accordance with the majority wish.

If an airplane is chartered to transport the press party, it should provide the comfort of a scheduled flight.

The aim in planning the arrangements should be to make the visit as convenient and as comfortable as possible for all those taking part. It should be remembered, for instance, that some people may prefer to come by car, particularly if they wish to go on elsewhere afterward. Occasionally one hears of press visits that appeared to have been planned more for the convenience of the staff than for those invited to attend!

The interest of a visit of this kind is often the opportunity provided for meeting the top-level executives of the company concerned as much as the actual visit to the facility. It is thus a good idea to try to arrange for top management to be well represented. Sometimes executives of the company are assigned to travel as hosts with the press, and this is always much appreciated. Apart from this consideration, hospitality demands that the guests should be welcomed at the assembly point by one or more members of staff who will accompany the party and iron out any difficulties that may arise.

A press visit is usually most successful when the party is restricted in number. It is often the practice, therefore, to have a series of press visits on successive days. One day may be allocated to photographers, the next to the national or state press, radio, and television, and the following day to the trade and technical press. This arrangement makes more demands on staff time, but it is likely to result in much better press coverage.

On many press visits the careful planning is undone by insufficient attention to the choice and briefing of the guides. This is one of the most important parts of the whole operation and it deserves more attention than it sometimes receives.

Even when there are sufficient guides available for the parties to be restricted to six or seven people in each, it is still essential for the guides to try to find a quiet spot when they are imparting information. Usually they try to shout over the noise of the machines. This point presents real difficulties, but it should be possible to talk about the machine or process in a quieter spot before coming right into the worst of the din. Where the parties are larger, the whole matter becomes almost impossible: One solution is to install a microphone at one or more vantage points, or for the guides to carry a megaphone or simple public address equipment.

The guides should have badges bearing their names so that they may be identified easily. A simple but effective way of assigning the press to their parties should be worked out beforehand; often much time is wasted on what should be a simple maneuver, and nothing is more frustrating than milling around waiting to be formed into groups.

When there is a general press visit, the party may be a very large one and may include local, state, regional and even national and international press representatives as well as editors from the trade and technical press. In such circumstances it is often the practice to group together journalists of like interests when dividing up into smaller groups for touring purposes. This results, for example, in all the electrical press representatives finding themselves in the same group. The reasoning behind this is that the guide can be someone qualified to answer difficult or complex questions of an electrical nature. There is, however, a serious snag about this arrangement, since the keen technical journalist is likely to be inhibited in his questioning by the realization that his closest competitors will also hear the answers—noise of machines permitting.

There are a number of criticisms that apply to many press facility visits. It is usual and desirable for the managing director, the works manager, or some other knowledgable executive of the company to welcome the press, but the speech should be kept short, especially when time is limited.

It is also usually desirable for a general session to be held again at the conclusion of the tour for a final question-and-answer period, possibly with refreshments. Some visits are a positive feat of endurance. The itinerary should be restricted to a reasonable length, especially if it is physically strenuous. It is not a good idea to hand out large amounts of literature that must be carried around during the tour. A way of solving the problem is to wait until the end of the tour before making materials or a press kit available. However, many reporters will want to study the materials en route. The best solution, therefore, may be to make the materials available at the outset and then arrange a place where reporters can leave the materials if they wish to do so during the tour.

Photographs of the main press-tour features should be made available. The usual practice is to include a few prints in every press kit folder and to show other photographs which can be provided upon request. It would be a good idea if some attempt was made to provide exclusive photographs even on mass visits. This can be achieved if a sufficient number of photographs are taken from different angles and only one print issued of each.

PRESS ARRANGEMENTS AT CONFERENCES

Each year an organization may hold many luncheons, dinners, meetings, and conferences that are not intended primarily for the press but from which valuable publicity can result if journalists are invited to attend and given facilities for reporting the proceedings. The occasions range from political meetings to annual conferences of learned and scientific bodies. In all instances it is desirable for one responsible official to be given the duty of looking after the press and seeing that they receive—in advance, where possible—copies of the program, agenda, and other relevant documents. The press should be informed in advance as to the name of this contact. Whenever possible he should keep himself free of other duties so that he is available to assist the press—for example, by explaining the procedure, identifying speakers, and generally giving any help the press requires.

It is customary at meetings to provide tables and chairs for the press in a position where they can see and hear clearly. The tables are often immediately in front or at the side of the platform, but in deciding where to place the press it should be borne in mind that they may wish to go out and telephone their stories during the sessions. If adequate telephones are not available nearby, it is necessary to arrange for extra temporary installations. If the conference lasts more than one day, the journalists will appreciate having a special press room which they can make their headquarters.

When the conference is a highly technical one, it is a good plan to arrange daily briefing meetings for the press at which the chairman or other appropriate official discusses the day's proceedings and is prepared to answer questions. Such meetings help the nontechnical journalist to avoid mistakes when writing his reports.

LETTERS TO THE EDITOR

A time-honored and effective way of achieving public attention for a point of view is by using the correspondence columns of newspapers or periodicals. Most editors welcome letters for publication and do not mind the writer expressing partisan views.

Letters to the editor can be grouped into three categories. The letter may comment on a topic of public or private concern, continue an existing correspondence, or comment or complain about a previously published item in the paper. The letter should be composed with care and should be tailored to suit the style of the journal to which it is sent.

When a letter is written to correct a misstatement or ambiguity it is particularly important not to repeat the original error, as this will give it a new currency and may bring it to the notice of many readers who may have missed its original publication. This is a point not sufficiently appreciated even by many experienced practitioners.

Judgment should be exercised in deciding the signature of a letter written on behalf of a company or organization. In general, it is preferable that the letter should be signed by the top executive most closely concerned with the subject. This is particularly wise when the letter is apologizing for inconvenience caused to the public. Such excuses come much better from the chief executive than from the public relations officer.

Major metropolitan newspapers publish only a very small percentage of the letters received. Small daily newspapers, however, will print any letter that is relevant or of general or local interest.

Editors will usually print a letter expressing the opposite point of view, particularly when it is signed by a chief executive. A call to the editor bringing to his attention that the letter is being sent is a good idea. However, pressure or threats of any type will do much more harm than good. It is very rare for newspapers to publish a correction, but most editors will agree to print a letter of explanation even if it is a long and technical one.

In general, of course, letters to the editor should be kept very brief and to the point. If a letter is long it runs the risk of being edited, and this may affect some of the main points of the letter. If the subject is an important one it is wise to ask that the letter not be altered or shortened without the writer's prior agreement.

On matters of general public interest it is possible to secure nation-wide publicity by means of letters to the editor if the letters are tailored to suit each publication.

A letter published in a major newspaper will often have very wide repercussions, and the possibility of wide publicity for a letter to the editor is good reason for ensuring that the facts are absolutely true. It is equally essential that the signature of the letter should be genuine. To submit letters for publication under an assumed signature is unethical.

ASSESSING PRESS ACTIVITY

A media relations office should keep a close watch on everything that appears in the press that has a direct or indirect bearing on the organization's interests. This will be both to assess the result of any positive press activity carried out and to watch for reports of interest or any that criticize the organization.

The monitoring of the press is a massive undertaking, and it is usual to subscribe to a press clipping service that will undertake this work for a fee. However, no press clipping service is infallible, and it is often desirable to subscribe to two or more services in order to achieve as complete a coverage as possible. It helps the clipping service to be more thorough if they are sent copies of press releases issued and are told in advance of special events of particular interest.

In large industries and organizations which come into daily contact with the public and with public opinion, it is usually considered necessary to monitor the press within the organization each day. Press clippings are copied and circulated to top management officials.

The press officer should keep records of all press clippings received. When there has been a special function, such as the opening of a new building, it is a good plan to develop a scrapbook of all clippings relating to the function. The press clippings should include the name of the newspaper or magazine, the date, and the location in the newspaper or periodical in which they were published.

Videotape and recording equipment are now making it possible also to monitor the broadcast media for later review by top management. This practice is becoming more feasible with advancements in the technology and the lower cost of the process resulting from mass production of the equipment.

SUMMARY

There may be no obligation on an organization to have any dealings with the press, but if its activities are of public interest the press will publish reports and comment whether they receive the cooperation of those concerned or not. If they do receive help, there is less likelihood of garbled reports or inaccurate information which can cause embarrassment. In addition, there are many opportunities for securing useful publicity, some of which have been outlined in this chapter.

Even in small organizations, a responsible person should be designated to act as the press contact. He or she should educate himself or herself as to how the press works and how an organization can maintain good relations with the press.

In large organizations, the job of press officer is a full-time responsibility, and competent, experienced individuals should be appointed to the position and provided with adequate staff and support.

Although press clippings give an indication of results, they cannot provide reliable quantitative measurement, for the reasons given in Chapter 1.

4

The Printed Word

The printed word is the most important medium of communication between any organization and the outside world. The subject of press relations was dealt with in Chapter 3, but there remains the great variety of printed material an organization produces for both internal and external use.

The printed matter will include office forms, invoices, letterheads, and items of this nature which have little relevance to public relations, except that there is a great deal to be said for adopting a uniform image for the firm. A large organization may have an internal business office assigned the responsibility of ordering equipment and supplies. The public relations staff, however, should be given the opportunity of making suggestions on the style and design of most printed items. In a small organization it is desirable that all printed matter be the responsibility of the public relations staff.

STYLE AND DESIGN

To look at a magazine published over thirty years ago is to notice the great changes that have occurred since then in the use of typefaces and the style of illustrations. This is particularly striking in the case of the advertisements, which often lead the way in design. One becomes accustomed to contemporary print design from advertising seen on all sides and from packaging design, and it is a fallacy to think that the average man or woman is not influenced by the appearance of printed matter presented to him or her.

Many organizations have adopted a house style that has become so well known that their products or advertisements are recognized instantly. The house style may consist of a logo, a particular typeface, a special color, or a combination of these factors. A house style is used to good effect by most international organizations.

A well-designed house style will lend itself to modification so that it can be used effectively on items differing as widely as letterheads and delivery vans. If an organization publishes a wide variety of items— including company reports, house journals, catalogs, and reference books—it would be inappropriate for all these publications to have the same typography or cover design, but there is much to be gained from having a recognizable family relationship common to all publications.

The design of print is only one example of how it is possible to project the character of an organization in such a way that it is readily recognizable by the public. The intelligent use of good design in every- thing an organization does—its buildings, its products, its publications, and so on—can do much to create an overall image which, if supported with sound policies, can do much in securing public approval.

KNOWING ABOUT DESIGN

It is unnecessary for those in public relations to possess an expert knowledge of design, but it is essential to understand that design matters. In simple words, it means the organization of the printed page and its effect on the reader. The success of printed material will depend on the success of its design. As in other branches of craftsmanship, taste will vary considerably, and it may be difficult to secure agreement on what is *good* design; but there should be less difficulty in recognizing and extirpating *bad* design. Here again, however, taste varies with time and with geographical location, and it would be wrong for the public rela- tions adviser to try to ride roughshod over the likes and dislikes of his management. Rather it is his duty to educate and to interest others in design, and thus to obtain the opportunity to make experiments in the use of print.

Only organizations that produce a large number of publications can afford to have their own graphic experts, so it is customary to use the services of a freelance designer with a special interest in the graphic arts. Often one uses several different designers to achieve a greater variety of ideas. An experienced designer is an expert in graphic design, but an experienced public relations practitioner knows the effect he is trying to achieve and should not be afraid of backing his own opinion against the views of the designer.

A number of specialist companies have sprung up that offer an advisory and publishing service in rather the same way that a film-producing company makes films. If they are fully briefed on the object of the publication, the readers to whom it is addressed, the budget, and so on, they will prepare suggestions and, when these are approved, carry through the production right to the final delivery, whether it is a publicity leaflet, a prestige booklet, or a history of the firm. Some of these companies do excellent work, and this method of dealing with publications is to be recommended in those cases where the public relations department is too small to handle its own publication design and preparation.

WORKING WITH THE PRINTER

Public relations brings one into constant contact with printers, and although a professional knowledge of printing is not necessary, it is essential to have a good working knowledge of printing processes and methods. Without this background knowledge one cannot argue with the printer or assess critically the advice of designers whose enthusiasm sometimes may run away with them, without due regard for what is practicable or economical.

There are many good books on the history and practice of printing, and most printers will be willing to show you their printing operation. Visiting a number of different printers is one of the best ways to acquire a basic knowledge of printing, and these visits give an opportunity to make a critical appraisal of the manner in which the various printers organize their work. There is no doubt that printers prefer to work with clients who know something about the craft, but it is foolish to try to hoodwink them by pretending to know more than one actually does.

There are three main factors in obtaining printing services: cost, service, and quality of the finished work. As in most things, one tends to get the quality of printing for which one is prepared to pay. Printers fall into different price categories based on the degree of service the customer expects to receive. The best printers provide a design service, an extremely wide range of typefaces, a high standard of proofreading, and do everything possible to make printing effortless for the customer. A printer in one of the lowest price categories, however, does not have any proofreaders—the foreman does what reading there is—and the client has to exercise the utmost care to ensure that the final result is satisfactory. Between these extremes there is every variety, and the secret is to find a printer whose service and standards are high but whose prices are reasonable.

Service covers a number of points. It is desirable to be able to contact the printer quickly. Therefore, location in the same city or area is preferable. A printer plans his work in rotation, but should be willing to work overtime to print an item that is needed on short notice. One is entitled to expect that a printer will provide a time schedule for a job and keep to it provided he receives the copy on time and there is no undue delay in reading proofs.

A well-conceived publication can fail in its objective if it is poorly printed or contains typographical errors. For this reason it is usually false economy in public relations to seek the lowest price for printing. The practice of inviting bids for every print job is not recommended for it puts unnecessary work on printers' estimating departments and interferes with the establishment of a continuing relationship with a printer that enables him to provide the best service. One should always invite bids for printing a new house journal or major publication, but for job printing it is wiser to know one's printer and to trust him to charge a fair price. The ideal arrangement is to use several printers, choosing the one most suitable for each particular job. When the staff at a printer know you, they will usually put that little extra effort into the work they are doing for you to ensure a first-class result.

There can be no condoning of bad printing. Advance copies of any publication should be inspected, and if there are any serious errors or blemishes they should be corrected before the job is issued even if it means reprinting some the pages. If the printer is responsible for the errors there should not be any extra charge. Even if it means paying extra, every effort should be made to achieve a perfect result if the publication is an important one. To have to include an errata slip in a publication is an admission of incompetency.

The most costly mistake in printing is to change one's mind at the proof stage. Unfortunately, some of those in authority do not seem capable of knowing what they wish to say until they see it actually in print, and many people are unable to resist the temptation to alter a proof. These last-minute changes are not only very costly but may often jeopardize the delivery date.

It is necessary to watch very carefully charges made by printers for "authors' corrections." A printer should be prepared to justify these charges.

The most successful printing job will not necessarily be the one that was printed regardless of cost. In fact it is as much a solecism to overdress a publication as it is to overdress oneself. The style and quality of a publication should be chosen so that it is in keeping with the function it is intended to perform.

KEEPING ABREAST OF MODERN
PRINTING METHODS

Letterpress has been the generally accepted method of printing for over five hundred years, but its supremacy is now being challenged by photogravure and offset lithography.

Linocuts and woodcuts are other examples of the relief method which is the basis of letterpress. The type or printing stereos and blocks are raised above the surface and receive the printing ink, which is transferred to the paper. Letterpress gives a crisp, clear impression, and the type can be set by machine, making it the method of choice for all printing containing a considerable amount of text. Modern developments in letterpress have included the introduction of the electronic scanning method of making blocks and the introduction of phototypesetting, which takes the place of metal type.

In photogravure the process is an intaglio one, that is, the printing areas are below the nonprinting areas, as in engraving and etching processes. The ink fills the recesses in the surface, and as the printing takes place the ink is sucked up out of the recess onto the paper, giving opacity and depth of color.

Lithography is a planographic process, meaning that the printing surface is flat. The printing areas are treated so that they accept the ink, while the nonprinting areas of the surface reject the ink. Lithography is based on the principles that grease and water do not mix. There is no relief surface to give a sharp edge to the ink, so the result usually has a typical softness.

Photogravure is particularly suitable for high-quality four-color printing, but it is only economical if the runs are substantial.

Screen process printing is a stencil type of operation and was originally known as silkscreen printing. This term is no longer accurate, as silk bolting cloth is not the only material used today. Ink is squeezed through the openings of a selectively blocked-out fabric, and an amazing variety of different inks can be employed in this type of printing. Screen printing is used extensively for posters, printing onto metal and other materials, and for printing textiles and wallpapers.

A newer development is the increasing popularity of office offset machines. Where there is a considerable amount of office printing to be done, such as forms, internal memoranda, or information booklets, the installation of an office offset machine is an economical addition, and it provides facilities for printing items very quickly when the occasion demands. There are many different kinds of offset machines on the market, and some of the more elaborate models can do excellent printing. Many printers are now using them exclusively.

The term *web offset* in printing can be defined as a process that transfers an image from a rubber blanket onto a continuous web (roll) of paper. This development of the lithographic process has established itself during recent years and has replaced letterpress and rotary machines for the printing of many magazines and newspapers. It provides high-speed printing of good quality, in monochrome or color.

Computer typesetting is making steady progress and is particularly suitable for directories or yearbooks, as it is easy to update the text each year and to incorporate alterations and additions. Its extension to general printing has been slower, but computer typesetting is used successfully by an increasing number of newspapers.

PRINTING PAPER

The choice of the right paper is important in securing a first-class result. The paper should be chosen in the light of the desired effect. In certain types of publications, a rough paper or a cartridge paper may be much more effective than a coated or art paper. If you buy your paper direct, the paper manufacturer's representative will be glad to advise you on the selection of paper; but also discuss the question with your printer, as he has to print on the paper!

Sometimes it is a good idea to have a specimen page proofed on different types of paper before making the final choice. It can be very difficult to match the exact house style color when using different types of printing papers.

Paper is made in a number of standard sizes, and to have special sizes made is a costly procedure. It is desirable to bear this point in mind when planning a publication. The ideal is to have a paper size that permits blocks to bleed but does not leave much paper to be cut off when trimming to size.

HOUSE JOURNALS

One of the well-established media of public relations is the house journal. This title is to be preferred to the older "house magazine," even though the purist will point out that few, if any, house journals are published daily!

The usual definition of a house journal is that it is a nonprofit-making periodical publication published by an organization to maintain contact with its employees or with the public. House journals vary in size, style, and type so greatly that it is usual to classify them by their readership. They are either published for internal consumption, for external distribution, or for a combination of the two.

"Internals" may be intended for all of an organization's employees, or for certain factories or other specialized groups. "Externals" may be general prestige publications, or directed at specific sections of the public, customers, dealers, and so on. It is almost impossible to pinpoint the readership of the dual-purpose house journal, and this is the weakness of this type of publication.

Some editors of house journals may feel they are performing a function that is outside the public relations program of the organization. It is true that an internal house journal plays an important part in personnel relations, but many aspects of public relations impinge on the field of personnel relations, and in all large organizations there is a constant need for close liaison between those working in these allied fields.

In a large organization, the editor of the house journal is likely to be engaged full time in preparation of the journal; but in smaller companies, or where the house journal appears quarterly or even less frequently, it is likely to be the responsibility of the public relations department.

A journal inevitably reflects the personality of the editor, and if the editor understands the journal's purpose and the role the publication has in an organization's public relations program, there is no reason for interference. The right time to criticize is after an issue has appeared, when comments and views are useful in helping to shape future issues. It has never been possible to edit successfully by committee, and it never will produce a successful result. The classic example is the editor of a house journal who had to report to a works committee of thirty-two persons. Each article had to be completely read to the committee, who took the opportunity of criticizing nearly every word. Fortunately for the sanity of the editor in question, a different method was adopted later!

Generalizations are notoriously misleading, and this is particularly true when considering house journals. No two journals have the same background, and the aims and objectives vary considerably according to the circumstances of the organization. In the case of "internals" there are a number of controversial points which arouse heated discussion. Should employees pay for the house journal, and if so, how much? Should the journal be distributed at work, or should it be sent to the homes of employees? Should payment be made to employees who contribute articles or items of news? Should each issue include a policy statement from the chief executive? To what extent should humor—

and pinups—be allowed? These are a few of the questions that have to be decided when planning an internal house journal; but there are no ready-made answers, for many approaches have proven successful.

The main purpose of an employee journal is to foster a family feeling by taking the workers and staff into the confidence of management, explaining policies, and seeking their interest and cooperation. This would make a dull journal—however cleverly it was interpreted—unless it were supplemented by more general reading and by a full cover of staff activities. House journals present wonderful opportunities for imaginative editing, hampered only by the need usually to keep within a fairly tight budget, and it is a pity that so few editors rise fully to the occasion. The best internal house journals are excellent, but the general standard is still mediocre.

The majority of employee journals are booklet size, but a few have used the newspaper format very successfully. Where the print order is fairly large and the main object of the journal is the provision of news and information, the newspaper style deserves careful consideration.

When a house journal has become established, management often wants to send complimentary copies to local and state officials, to customers, and to others who come into regular contact with the organization. Provided the standard of the journal is high, there is no reason why this wider distribution should not be permitted. The danger, however, is that this wide distribution may lead to pressures on the editor to modify the editorial policy. This leads to a vain attempt to satisfy two different types of readership, and usually to a deterioration in the standard of the journal.

Some internal-external journals have proven successful, but usually when the difficulties inherent in this type of journal have been faced squarely from the outset. It must be recognized that it is far better to have separate house journals to meet the needs of the internal and external readership. Apart from editorial aspects, it is likely to prove cheaper to have two separate journals than to publish an internal-external journal.

The external prestige house journal is approaching and in many cases has reached the quality demanded in the commercial periodical publishing field, and is in fact an example of a controlled circulation magazine—but published to promote public relations rather than to attract advertising support.

DIRECT MAIL

Leaflets, pamphlets, broadsides, letters, and telegrams have often had a profound effect, and have at times changed the course of history. They remain a very effective medium of communication and often find a place in a public relations campaign.

It may be a question of sending out a few dozen letters, or several thousand, but the principles are the same. The letter must appear to be a personal communication, and the recipient must feel that it has a message for him. The wording should be to the point and free from ambiguity. The letter may be printed by one of the methods that closely resemble the effect of typewriting, but it should be addressed to the person for whom it is intended and signed individually. A letter with a printed or rubber-stamped signature loses any possibility of being regarded as a personal communication and is unlikely to receive a good response.

Opinion is divided as to whether better results are obtained from a very short letter—on one side of the sheet—or from a longer letter, which can give more information and thus arouse a greater degree of interest. There is agreement, however, that it is always desirable to follow up the first communication by others if anything useful is to be achieved.

It is always wise to make it easy for the recipient to do what is requested. More replies can be expected if it is only a matter of making a few check marks on a questionnaire, and if an addressed envelope is enclosed, than if it is necessary to write a letter in reply.

Direct-mail advertising has been developed to a high degree, and many of the techniques can be adopted when communicating through the mail for public relations purposes.

5

Photography as an Aid
to Public Relations

In the chapter dealing with press relations some comments were made on the provision of photographs for the press at conferences and on facility visits. The use of photography in public relations deserves special attention, as many people do not realize the full potentialities of photographs.

The first point to appreciate is that photographs always lend authenticity. Everyone knows that photographs can be as misleading as statistics, but nevertheless they are generally accepted as authentic proof of facts or events.

Good photographs have a compelling appeal that is absent from printed matter, however well laid out and displayed. Few publications are found these days in which photographs and other types of illustrations are absent, for it has become generally accepted that photographs add to the interest and stimulate close attention. This is now true even of such publications as companies' annual reports, which were formerly austere documents but are now usually illustrated.

QUALITY OF PHOTOGRAPHY

The word *good* used in the opening sentence of the last paragraph is very important. As photographs have become accepted as a suitable embellishment to all types of printed matter, the reading public has become more critical of the quality of photographs and the skill with which they are presented. Fortunately, improved types of film and better understanding of camera techniques and printing methods have resulted in vastly improved results being achieved by professional photographers. A closer study of technique and lighting as a part of academic training, and the wide development of photography in industry, have resulted in a much higher standard of entrant to the profession.

Public relation practitioners should demand a high standard from the photographers they use, and not be content with anything less. Just as a good photograph enhances a story, so does a poor one depreciate its effect. A good policy is to demand the best possible photographs and to refuse to use poor ones. In certain instances where it is essential to use a poor-quality photograph, and it is not possible to acquire a replacement, retouching may be a recourse—but this should only be done as a last resort, as retouching tends to give an artificial appearance.

USES OF PHOTOGRAPHS

1. To illustrate news stories that are to appear in newspapers or the technical press.
2. To illustrate reports, booklets, house journals, and so on.
3. For record purposes.
4. For use in advertisements or posters.
5. For training and research.

Advertising photography is outside the scope of this book. Some of the results achieved in this field are works of art; even today, however, some photographs used in advertisements are poor in quality. Photographs for record purposes are very important, but present little technical difficulty since the purpose is to achieve an exact likeness. Photographs for news purposes or for use in publications are another matter: Here there is endless opportunity for ingenuity and art.

PHOTOGRAPHY AT SPECIAL EVENTS

The most effective way to achieve editorial photographic publicity for an event such as an exhibition, an opening of a building, or a conference, is to issue a general invitation to the press. It is often desirable to invite press photographers to attend earlier than the general press preview, as this gives them better photographic opportunities. They will probably wish to attend the official opening as well.

It is also wise to arrange for a staff or commercial photographer to cover it fully for the organizers rather than to rely on results of photographers who might attend. This method also takes care of the copyright problem, for if you commission and pay for the photographs you can then use them in any way you wish.

PHOTOGRAPHS AS NEWS STORIES

The press will often use photographs which tell a story, for example, the chief executive leaving on a trip to China, a very large piece of equipment being shipped to South America, a presentation to a worker who has completed fifty years' service, a foreign engineers visitation, and so on. The essential points are—

1. They must be striking and interesting photographs.
2. They must be topical.
3. They must be adequately captioned.
4. Every picture should tell a story; if in addition it is pleasing aesthetically, the value is increased.

Photographs of this kind provide very useful editorial publicity, and often one photograph appears in a great variety of publications at home and overseas. Some organizations achieve much more success in this field than others due to the quality of the prints submitted. Sometimes, however, excellent prints arrive in editorial offices in poor condition due to failure to protect them properly. Prints are often spoiled by unwise use of paper clips or by writing on the reverse side with a ballpoint pen or hard pencil.

PHOTOGRAPHS FOR PUBLICATIONS

When photographs are needed for publications, it is possible to plan ahead and thus to achieve better results than are always possible in the case of photographs of news events where immediacy is the first essential. The industrial photographer is able to illustrate not only what is going on in industry, but also something of its life and spirit. This is creative art, and there are many fine photographers who are achieving results that can be used to great effect in a public relations program. Photographs can be used very effectively in exhibitions and trade fairs in the form of very large transparencies or prints.

The best industrial photographers take their work very seriously and like to have adequate time to plan their pictures. It is unrealistic to expect a photographer to walk into a factory and be able to decide immediately on the shots that will best express the spirit of the place. A good photographer will be able to achieve results on the spur of the moment, but he will undoubtedly achieve better photographs if he has the time to look around and to plan a series of pictures that will tell the story to the best advantage. This will involve not only a study of the appearance of different parts of the plant, but also talking to some of the personnel and trying to understand something of the living tradition of the job.

Most photographers will want to include people in their photographs to add human interest to what might otherwise be an inanimate shot or to provide the viewer with a comparison of size. When individuals are included, they will naturally want to look their best, but steps should be taken to assure that the clothing and gear worn is normal for the situation and not contrived or artificial. Compliance with safety regulations is also of importance, and many corporations will not permit the use of a photograph in which safety regulations were ignored for aesthetic reasons.

In black and white photography the effect depends mainly on the dramatic use of light and shade. It is the artistic use of lighting that gives a picture its hidden power, and this applies to flash as well as natural lighting. The indiscriminate use of a single flashbulb on the camera should be discouraged, owing to the inferior results obtained by this method. The use of flashbulbs is sometimes dangerous if, for example, there are fumes in the air which may ignite. This is a point that should be watched, as accidents have occurred.

Most top-rank industrial photographers insist on printing their own photographs so that they can control the quality, which can make or mar the results of their camera work. Using qualified and competent professional photographers is fairly expensive, but using those whose results cannot be published with pride is often more costly.

Many companies employ their own photographers, and some of them achieve excellent results. Too often, however, the staff photographer is inadequately paid and grossly overworked. He is sometimes expected to do all the clerical and administrative work in addition to operating the darkroom and taking all the photographs. If a concern is large enough to need its own staff photographer, it should be prepared to budget for adequate professional and supporting staff.

Staff photographers should be given every encouragement to do good work and to improve their skill. No public relations department can afford to have a poor photographer on its staff, but a person showing promise of making a good photographer should be given every opportunity of realizing his or her potential.

PHOTOGRAPHIC LIBRARIES

In some instances it is more satisfactory to obtain a photograph from a photographic library than to endeavor to have pictures taken specially. This is, of course, essential when dealing with events that are past history. Fortunately, there is a wide variety of libraries that can supply photographs on almost every subject.

Most large industrial companies maintain their own photographic libraries, and will usually be very willing to supply prints for use subject to suitable acknowledgment. In some cases they will even take photographs especially to meet requests.

Finally, mention should be made of the photographic libraries of newspapers and many periodicals.

SECURING THE BEST RESULTS FROM PHOTOGRAPHY

There are seven main points to watch:

1. Secure the best photographer for the particular type of assignment. It is more useful to have a few photographs by an expert than many by a less brilliant exponent.

2. Give the photographer a careful briefing on the type of photographs required. It is necessary to tell him what shots to take, but the best results will come from giving him a fairly free hand. He will often obtain striking and original results, even from most unpromising material.

3. Make sure that he has every facility for getting good results. Make sure that the factory manager knows that the photographer is coming, and why the photographs are needed, in order to secure his willing rather than grudging cooperation. Always go with the photographer yourself, or send a colleague who can ensure that the photographer is allowed all the time necessary to get good results. Unless the photographer secures friendly and willing cooperation from those with whom he is dealing, it is almost impossible for him to accomplish his job.

4. Ensure that all prints and negatives are adequately housed and catalogued for easy reference. When issuing photographs, always see that each print has a reference number and that it is adequately captioned. The caption should include the vital facts—who, where, why, or when—and as much additional information as possible. There is no need for the caption to be brief. The editor using the photograph will prefer to write his own short caption from the full details you supply. Attach the caption so that it hangs down in front of the print.

5. When using photographs in publications, take considerable trouble to ensure the best result by cropping the print. This may be done in order to alter the proportions of the photograph—for example, to fit a front cover—or to eliminate a blemish or extraneous object, or to concentrate attention on a particular section of the photograph. Intelligent

cropping of a photograph can work wonders. Sometimes it is helpful to consult the photographer about the trimming of a print, for he may have a little more on the negative; and with his knowledge of composition he can possibly help to suggest the most effective manner of making the reproduction.

6. Carefully examine photographs to make sure that there are no old tin cans, trailing wires, or other accidental and unwanted extras in the picture. If blemishes of this type cannot be eliminated by cropping, artistic retouching may solve the problem.

6

Exhibitions
and Trade Shows

Modern exhibitions and trade shows have become an accepted medium of public relations and trade promotion. There is no clear demarcation between an exhibition and a trade show, and the terms are interchanged freely. A trade show, however, as its name implies, is staged for the purpose of selling goods or demonstrating new ideas and techniques. An exhibition, on the other hand, may range from a prestige international show such as a world fair, to small educational displays in a local public library or factory cafeteria.

In most organizations the public relations department is responsible for all types of exhibitions, so the subject of exhibiting is discussed here in general terms.

Exhibiting breaks down into three responsibilities:

1. Deciding which exhibitions to support, and to what degree, or which invitations for exhibits to accept.
2. Preparing a plan, and organizing the construction of the exhibit.
3. Staffing and controlling the exhibit. This will include the period prior to the opening and during the dismantling or storage.

CHOOSING THE EXHIBITIONS
TO SUPPORT

In any industry certain exhibitions will be considered the important ones to support, but beyond these there is considerable scope for making the right or wrong choice.

In many instances, the decision to support a particular exhibition may be up to the chief executive or the governing board; but the public relations adviser should be asked for an opinion, and he should be competent to express a useful view on a question that is likely to involve considerable expenditure. It is difficult to judge the value of an exhibition without having visited it at least once, and therefore every opportunity should be taken of going to exhibitions and trade fairs of interest to your organization.

There are several points on which information is needed in making a decision as to participation. It is desirable to know the exact scope of the exhibition, the size of the attendance, and the type of visitors it attracts. Knowledge of the exhibiting conditions in an overseas exhibition will be useful in acquiring an idea of the expense likely to be involved.

In considering whether to support a particular trade show, it is likely that the sales department will have submitted their views on the sales likely to result from participation. There will thus be factual data on which to form a decision. It is more difficult to access the likely value of a prestige or public relations exhibit, and the decision is more likely to be based on opinion rather than on hard facts. Another point that often influences a decision to exhibit is the negative view that the company or organization cannot afford not to be represented when competitors will be present.

Thought should be given to whether the timing of the exhibition will permit adequate preparation, and whether it clashes with similar exhibitions taking place elsewhere.

The next question that arises is how much space is needed to display adequately the articles or services that are to be exhibited. Here the question of cost becomes a factor for, except in the case of small exhibits, the cost is more or less proportional to the floor space. A further complication is that in certain exhibitions it is necessary to reserve a large space in order to get an island site or a position on the ground floor. It is also necessary in some instances to exhibit regularly in order to qualify for a priority in exhibit-space allocation.

BUDGETING

Even simple exhibits are costly to construct, while prestige exhibits can be extremely expensive. Justification for the cost must be related to the effectiveness in reaching the intended audience and in conveying the desired message. Other factors will include the number of people who can be reached with the exhibit, publicity it may receive, and the durability and expected life of the exhibit.

The cost of preparing an exhibit will include designer and artist fees as well as the total cost of construction. This cost will be dependent upon the size of the exhibit, the materials used in construction, labor required in construction, the amount of photography and artwork, the lighting and electrical equipment required, the apparatus required for animation, video sound and computer equipment to be included, special effects desired, and so forth.

Although not included as a part of the exhibit construction budget, other costs that must be considered are transportation, assembly, exhibit space, insurance, security (if not provided), staffing (if needed), disassembly, storage in a climate-controlled environment, and repairs that may be required as the result of usage and transport wear and tear.

It is essential to draw up a careful budget and to do everything possible to keep the cost within the alloctaion. It is usual to allow a substantial sum, say ten percent, to cover contingencies.

PLANNING THE EXHIBIT

When planning an exhibit, the first step should be to determine how the exhibit will be viewed. Will it be viewed from a distance of three to five feet, for example, or will it be viewed from a much greater distance? Will there be large crowds viewing the exhibit or only a few individuals at a time? The answers to these questions will determine the size of the exhibit and the way in which it must be constructed for safety.

Who will view it? Will it be the public at large or more specialized groups such as potential stockholders, potential buyers, legislators, scientists, and so on. The type of group will affect the complexity of the information to be conveyed as well as the amount of information to be included.

The purpose of the exhibit must also be determined. Is it to inform, sell, create goodwill, help in changing or creating an image? Or is its purpose to attract large audiences, only a selected few, or to outpace competitors? The answer will determine the use of special attention-getting effects and help in deciding whether the exhibit must be manned for hospitality purposes. It will also determine whether the emphasis is to be placed on attractiveness or functional aspects.

It must also be known whether the exhibit is to have repeated usage. If it should, then it will be necessary to design it for easy disassembly, assembly, and transport. The durability and design for low maintenance will also be important.

The type of functions at which the exhibit may be used must also be known. For example, if outdoor usage is involved, the exhibit must be resistent to rain, sun, and wind damage. If the exhibit is to include special effects such as animation, lighting devices, computer equipment, slide shows, or rear-screen projection, the very use of some of these concepts will limit the facilities in which the exhibit can be placed and will also affect construction design.

All of these decisions must be determined and translated into specifications for guidance in design. Carefully written specifications will not only help the designer in providing a usable concept, but it will save time, help eliminate costly changes and errors, and help keep the project within the budget.

DESIGNING THE EXHIBIT

Unless an organization has its own experienced exhibition-design staff, it is recommended that the design and construction of the exhibit be contracted.

In order to provide a designer with guidance, a short one- or two-page brief should be written that conveys the message or messages that are to be projected by the exhibit. The brief should read like a short summary; it should be complete but extremely concise. It is the designer's job to relate the information in the brief to an audience through design, using the most effective visual and audio techniques possible within the specifications provided.

The designer will study the brief and specifications and may wish to visit the organization in order to view operations firsthand as well as to talk to some of the staff to obtain the feel of the organization's aims and policies. The designer will then present preliminary ideas which when agreed upon will become the plan for the exhibit. The process of reaching agreement with the designer is likely to be easier if he has been chosen with knowledge as to his or her design technique or approach. Most exhibition designers will tackle any type of exhibit; but some are more successful with particular subjects, and the public relations adviser is likely to be more in sympathy with the techniques of certain of the designers. It is therefore wise to make a point of finding out which designers have been responsible for exhibits at exhibitions which were particularly attractive and effective.

If the brief and specifications presented to the designer are adequate, he or she should be able to prepare an acceptable plan for the exhibit, bearing in mind the position of the exhibit in the exhibition hall and lighting.

When the exhibit is a large or complicated one, the designer should be required to supply a small scale model. This will give a clear impression of the details of the finished exhibit and will be very useful when discussing the exhibit with members of the organization unaccustomed to visualizing drawings in terms of three-dimensional display.

CONSTRUCTION OF THE EXHIBIT

Where time permits, the design plans and specifications should be submitted to two or three exhibit constructions firms for bids. The designer can suggest suitable firms; but there is a wide choice, and some of the smaller firms may be cheaper—although often at the expense of quality and service.

If the exhibition location is of a considerable distance, consideration must be given to on-site construction, or to construction of a major part of the exhibit for shipment. The nature of the overseas country in question, the availability of local labor, the type of exhibit, and the transportation costs will be some of the factors that will influence the decision on this point.

When the bids have been received, it is wise to make a decision quickly in order that the selected contractor can make an early start on any sections of the exhibit stand that are to be prefabricated. This is particularly essential in the case of overseas exhibitions, where transport may take a very long time. Furthermore, exhibitors who have found their exhibit stands only half ready at overseas exhibitions due to shipping strikes or port delays are likely to insist in the future that the schedule should be advanced to allow for such unexpected emergencies.

The designer's responsibilities do not end when the contract has been awarded to a contractor. It is his duty to supervise the construction and erection at all stages, and to commission the lettering, photographs, and so on; to order the furniture (usually rented); and to look after the thousand and one details inseparable from the arranging of an exhibition stand. In particular, the designer will study the rules and conditions of the exhibition in question, paying special attention to such points as permissible heights and weights, color schemes for fascias, rules regarding moving exhibits, live demonstrations, and so forth. If necessary, the designer will try to negotiate divergencies from these regulations where they are desirable for the success of the exhibit.

Organizations that exhibit frequently will probably have an exhibition department as a subsection of the public relations department. Where this does not apply, it is essential that one person should be given the responsibility for organizing and progressing the many details involved in exhibiting. One of the main duties will be keeping in close touch with the designer and the contractor. However capable and experienced the designer, it is wise for the representative of the client to take careful and close interest throughout and not be afraid of expressing an opinion.

The designer or his assistant will be on site during the erection and will ensure that the stand is completed in accordance with the specification—and in time for the opening! Keeping to the schedule can be extremely difficult, however, if there are any union troubles at the exhibition. Finally, after the exhibition is over the designer will check all the contractors' accounts, agree or disallow any extras, and certify the final accounts for payment. The savings from this alone may more than cover the designer's fees.

Mention has been made of exhibition rules and conditions. It is rare nowadays to find any objectionable clauses in these rules, but it is always wise to study them closely as they constitute the conditions of the contract between the exhibition organizers and the exhibitors. One point that has given rise to trouble in the past is the attempt by some organizers to retain moneys paid when the exhibition has had to be cancelled. It is now customary for a refund to be paid under such conditions, less a percentage to cover the promoters' reasonable costs.

DRAWING UP A TIMETABLE

There are so many details to be handled at various stages in the preparation for an exhibition that it is desirable to draw up a detailed timetable listing all the items that have to be attended to and giving the final dates in each case. The schedule will include such items as insurance, transport, briefing of staff, telephones, exhibit cleaning, photography of exhibit, preparation of literature, entries in the exhibition catalog, any advertising or other publicity, arranging press conferences, fire precautions, security, and possibly travel and accommodation for staff.

The time between deciding to exhibit and the actual opening day will vary considerably, but for a medium-sized exhibit about three to four months should be ample. If an exhibition is overseas, or if there are other complex factors involved, the preliminary planning may commence as much as a year before the opening date.

INSURANCE

The need to insure the exhibit is obvious, but it is also desirable to take out third-party insurance to cover any possible claims by members of the public who may trip over or injure themselves in any way when visiting the exhibit. Similarly, it is wise to take out insurance to cover the staff who will be manning the exhibit, and their personal effects.

TRANSPORTATION

Transportation may be fairly simple in the case of home exhibitions. but it becomes a most important aspect of exhibiting overseas. Even when an organization has its own shipping department, it is advisable to make transportation arrangements with one of the firms that specialize in providing transport and shipping for exhibitions. Otherwise there is a great deal of documentation to deal with, and possibly many complications in clearing the customs division of a particular country. A specialist firm has experience in meeting the peculiar problems that arise, and has methods of cutting red tape and short-circuiting complicated procedures.

STAFF TRAVEL AND ACCOMMODATION

It is usual to hand over the arrangements to a firm of travel agents with experience in the part of the world concerned. If a considerable number of staff are involved, however, it is sometimes preferable to rent housing facilities and to engage domestic staff. At overseas exhibitions it can be extremely difficult to acquire hotel accommodations in the same city as the exhibition and exhibitors often rent hotel accommodation in a nearby town. This is usually preferred to the alternative of lodging in private houses, which is quite expensive, but not very convenient. In all instances, the earlier the arrangements are made the more likely it is to be possible to acquire the needed arrangements. A reconnaissance on the spot is often the only satisfactory way of securing satisfactory accommodation.

LITERATURE

The type of exhibition will determine the advisability of preparing special literature for distribution, and whether it should be given out freely or only to selected visitors. Often a thin leaflet is prepared for wide distribution and a more detailed booklet for restricted issue. If the exhibition is overseas, it is essential that the printed material bear the name of the country of origin, and it may be necessary to pay duty in some countries even when it can be proved that it is to be distributed free of charge. The question of language may also arise: The utmost care should be taken to ensure the accuracy of any foreign language texts used.

The Exhibition Catalog

It is usual for exhibitors to be offered a free entry in the exhibition catalog, but the copy is often required several months ahead. In addition, it is often possible to have further entries on payment or to take displayed advertisements in the catalog. This question should receive proper attention, as entries in the appropriate sections of the catalog are very helpful.

ADVERTISING AND PUBLICITY

It may be considered advisable to advertise the company's participation in an exhibition in the trade press, the mass media, by posters, or by direct mail. Details of the exhibit should be sent, of course, to appropriate editors of the press in the hope of securing editorial mention.

PRESS CONFERENCES

Exhibition organizers usually invite the press to attend on the first morning, or on the previous day, and it is essential to be ready to receive the press on the exhibit premises on such occasions. In addition, it may be considered desirable to hold an individual press conference at an earlier date to give information about the exhibit. This is worthwhile only when the exhibit is a very special one or there are circumstances that warrant it. An exhibit prepared for an important overseas exhibition is sometimes set up in the home country for the benefit of the press.

At most exhibitions there is a press office where exhibitors can place press releases and other publicity material for visiting journalists to collect. Care should be taken to restock materials each day that the exhibition is open.

CLEANING, TELEPHONES, SECURITY

It is necessary to ensure that arrangements have been made for the cleaning of the exhibit area; for renting furniture, not forgetting ashtrays and wastepaper baskets; that fire requirements have been complied with; and that there are adequate security precautions. Telephones should be ordered, and arrangements made with a florist for flowers and indoor plants if desired.

STAFFING AND ADMINISTRATION OF THE STAND

The expenditure on an exhibition will be wasted unless adequate arrangements have been made for staffing and managing the exhibit during the show.

It is not possible to stipulate any optimum size for the staff, since it will depend on so many variables. In most cases it is desirable to have a few general staff plus sufficient technically or otherwise qualified personnel to deal with difficult questions. The location may also require multilingual staff. In planning the staff requirements it is necessary to allow for mealtimes and so on, and if the hours are very long it may be necessary to allow for twice the staff that are required to be on duty at any one time.

It is possible to hire exhibition staff from agencies that specialize in this field, but it is a good plan to build up one's own staff register of people who have proved absolutely reliable. As far as possible, it is wise to use staff from within the organization, since they are likely to be familiar with the background and also have a stake in the success of the exhibit. Irresponsible or negligent behavior of staff would jeopardize their future in the organization, so they are likely to be more trustworthy than employees taken on only for the duration of the exhibition.

Control of the exhibit must be vested in one person, with a reliable deputy. This person in control may be the same individual who has acted as the organizer of the exhibition, and this has the advantage that he or she will be familiar with every detail. This may not be possible if the organization has exhibits at other shows at the same time, and then it may be wise to choose the most reliable member of the exhibit staff. It is essential that this exhibit stand manager should be briefed in every detail and should be competent to control the behavior of the other exhibit staff. One of his or her jobs will be to prepare a staff roster and to see that punctuality is observed. Another obvious duty is to inspect the exhibit frequently for cleanliness and orderliness, and to take immediate action to remedy any damage or interference with the lighting or working models.

The need for adequate staff has been emphasized, but it is equally important that they should behave well. Too often a visitor to an exhibit finds it difficult to attract the attention of the attendants, who are standing in a corner engaged in earnest conversation. It is often useful to have a private office on the exhibit stand for talking with important visitors, but such an office is not intended for the staff to hide in. Teacups spread all over the exhibit area, staff lolling about with cigarettes hanging from their lips, staff chattering together or giggling or all going off to lunch together, are some of the mistakes that a competent exhibit manager will avoid.

At overseas exhibitions the interpreters may be locally engaged; when the stand is of a technical nature, it may be possible to engage the help of local students—provided there is adequate supervision.

DEALING WITH INQUIRIES

Everything possible should be done to encourage visitors to ask questions. Some exhibits are designed in such a way that the visitor has to make a positive effort to enter the exhibit area—have to step up on to a high platform, or having to search for the right part of the exhibit stand to enter. Any difficulty of this kind may reduce the likelihood of inquiries. When inquiries are made, they should be answered as fully as possible and details recorded so that in suitable cases the inquiry can be followed up from headquarters. A visitors' book for VIPs is also a desirable adjunct to an exhibit stand: People are usually flattered at being asked to sign the book, and it provides a useful reference for follow-up activities.

SOME POINTS TO WATCH

1. In many exhibition halls the general lighting is poor and it is therefore desirable to make sure that the exhibit illumination is adequate. Many fine exhibit designs are spoiled by lack of light.

2. It is generally accepted that an exhibit must tell its story three-dimensionally, and that text should be kept to a minimum. Unfortunately, some designers go further and always keep the size of the type to a minimum! Apart from the fact that visitors are unlikely to bother to read very small type, there may be many whose vision is inadequate.

3. Some exhibits are designed without any thought to storage space or rooms for hats and coats. It is always possible to make some suitable provision for this at the design stage, but it is not so easy when the exhibit stand has been completed.

4. Even when an exhibit is in a shell scheme it can be made to stand out by good design. Illumination and the wise use of color can prevent the boxlike appearance that is often a failing of shell schemes.

5. A good exhibit is wasted if it is not visited. It is necessary, therefore, to devote considerable thought to methods of securing the attendance of those likely to be interested. The promoters of the exhibition will publicize it in general terms, and this should be backed up by sending invitations to suitable people—not forgetting universities and technical colleges, women's organizations, and similar sources of likely visitors.

6. If an exhibit is on the ground floor and is visible from the balcony, care should be taken to see that the appearance of the top of the stand is not untidy, as this can make a very bad impression.

7. It is usually necessary to obtain permission from the organizers for any flashing signs, noisy machinery, or any other features that may interfere with the comfort of nearby exhibitors. It is also always wise to contact, at an early stage, the exhibitors who have adjacent exhibit locations to avoid undue clash in style or color.

8. Photographs of the exhibit are useful for publicity and record purposes. It is usually rather difficult to get really good photographs of an exhibition stand, and it is therefore wise to use a professional photographer in preference to a press or agency one. Photographs of exhibits are often taken at night, as it may be impracticable to photograph the completed exhibit before the exhibition opens and it is likely to be difficult for the photographer to work properly while the exhibition is open. In addition to photographs of the exhibit stand, it is desirable to make arrangements for news pictures to be taken when VIPs visit the stand.

9. Pilfering is always a problem at public exhibitions, but the most dangerous time is after the exhibition finishes and before dismantling actually commences. There have been cases when a large and valuable carpet has been stolen even though the actual exhibit was on top of it!

10. It is essential to do nothing at an exhibition that might conflict with union regulations, as any infringement may cause a strike of the whole labor force in the exhibition.

11. If it is intended to dispense hospitality on the exhibit stand, it is necessary to see that proper facilities for this are included in the design. It is desirable that the bar and entertaining area should be screened from public view. In some exhibitions the dispensing of alcoholic beverages on exhibit locations is not allowed.

12. The electrical wiring plan for the exhibit should cover all likely needs, not forgetting a point for the vacuum cleaner if the exhibit area is carpeted. Often a fan for cooling or heating is essential, as temperatures may run to extremes.

13. When an exhibit is stored for future use, temperature and humidity control is essential to prevent warping, deterioration of paint, photographs, lettering, and so forth.

14. If an exhibit is to be repeatedly used in different locations, design for ease in movement and shipment are important. Exhibits that require

a full crew of men to move and reassemble increase costs and complicate staffing needs.

EXHIBITING COLLECTIVELY

There are many advantages if companies can exhibit collectively overseas. It can increase the impact, and therefore improve results, while at the same time reduce the cost to all participants. The U.S. Department of Commerce aids in organizing such opportunities in conjunction with a trade association or chamber of commerce.

It is often difficult to assess the value of participation in a particular exhibition or trade fair, but many exhibitors sell the equipment they display, which covers their costs—apart from other longer-term results. In a nunmber of countries special quotas or allocations of foreign currency are made available for trade fairs, and this fact can make participation worthwhile for many companies.

An interesting way of assessing the value of participation in a trade fair is to equate the number of serious visitors to an exhibit stand with the cost of sending a salesman to visit *them*.

ORGANIZING A COMPLETE EXHIBITION

Most of this chapter has been devoted to considering the methods by which an organization provides an exhibit in an established exhibition. Sometimes the public relations department will be called upon to organize a complete exhibition, and this brings added responsibilities. The problem is mainly one of organization, for it is possible to engage the services of an architect-designer to advise on the layout and design of an exhibition and to act as the coordinating designer. The additional problems will include crowd control, reception of distinguished visitors, liaison with the police, providing a press office, attending to advance publicity, and keeping all exhibitors or divisions of your organization informed of arrangements.

The desirability—or otherwise—of a formal opening needs careful consideration. It is probably not necessary unless a really newsworthy personality can be secured to open the event. If an opening ceremony is held, check carefully on audibility of speeches.

Other special exhibiting problems arise if the organization is exhibiting at an agricultural show or at some other exhibition that takes place in the open air. In such cases it would be necessary to build a pavilion, possibly tented, unless mobile vehicles are used as a basis for the exhibit.

To go to the other extreme, an exhibition may take place in a public library. Here all that would be required might be some well-designed screens on which to display photographs, text, and other descriptive matter. Specially designed screens for use in this way are obtainable, and the cost is comparatively low. The smaller the exhibition, the more need there is for clean, decisive design that will make the most of available space but will not confuse the visitor by confronting him with a confused jumble of information.

Many small cities have poor exhibition facilities but some of the larger department stores are able to provide facilities for exhibitions to be held on their premises. Alternatively, it may be possible to secure suitable accommodation in a hotel. Many new hotels incorporate special exhibition and conference suites. Shopping malls and theaters also provide exhibition possibilities.

FEEDBACK FROM EXHIBITIONS

Many companies ignore the benefits that can accrue from bringing back from exhibitions photographs, videotape, or press reports that could be used in the company's house journal or publicity at home. Exhibitions should be regarded as part of a company's regular activities, not as isolated events.

7
The Film
in Public Relations

The film is a powerful medium of public relations, and its use dates back to the increasing popularity of the documentary film in the decade before World War II. The function of documentaries has been taken over to a great extent by television, but there is still a very important place for film in public relations as a medium of communication, instruction, marketing, research, and so on.

WHEN TO MAKE FILMS

It is not necessary for public relations personnel to be trained filmmakers, but it is necessary to have an adequate understanding of film technique in order to be able to advise on the use of film in an organization and to act as liaison with the film production company when a film is being made. It is sometimes necessary to support the producer against unreasonable demands for the inclusion of items that do not fit into the pattern of the film.

Films play an important part in teaching, education, training, and research, but it is their use in public relations that will be considered here.

Before embarking on filmmaking, it is essential to consider three fundamental points:

1. What is the objective of the film?
2. For what audience is the film intended and can this audience be reached successfully?
3. How much money can be spent on the film and its distribution, and could this money be spent to better advantage in other ways?

The public relations practitioner should be competent to advise in relations to these basic questions.

A film should be conceived in a very precise way. It must be aimed at a specific audience, with the intention of imparting information or putting over a particular point of view. Film has the power, shared only by television, of bringing audiences into direct communication with facts and ideas through the senses—sight and hearing—and the emotions. It is only worth making a film if the intended audience can be defined and if there is a reasonable prospect of being able to reach it. A small influential audience may sometimes justify the total expense of the film, but it is a true anomaly that films made specifically for a particular audience often have a surprising success with a much wider public. This possibility does not excuse the need to define audiences in advance.

The only way to acquire a critical appreciation of industrial films is to see as many different ones as possible. Industrial film festivals are held periodically in many countries, and provide an excellent opportunity of viewing a wide variety of public relations films and of comparing their production, direction, and presentation. The Public Relations Society of America hosts a film festival at its national convention each year at which award winners are announced.

ASSESSING THE AUDIENCE

The audience to be reached is either the general public through the commercial cinema or television (the theatrical audience), or other audiences, which are classified as nontheatrical audiences. These two groups of audiences will react better to different methods of approach, and often require different techniques in film production. It is comparatively rare that a film will prove equally successful for these two types of audience, but it is sometimes feasible to make two different versions of the same film.

Theatrical Audiences

Television audiences can be reached in two ways: either by advertising films where the showing time is bought from the commercial television company, or by feature films of general interest that may be acceptable to both the National Educational Television Network, and to the commercial television contractors. Educational television stations are usually prepared to show good-quality documentary films, but they insist that there be no direct advertising and that any reference to the sponsor be indirect and incidental.

Documentary films planned for movie theater audiences are reached in the same way although the use of the films by commercial theaters has become a rarity.

Nontheatrical Audiences

Most public relations films are made with nontheatrical audiences in mind. Such audiences can be grouped into two main categories.

Existing Audiences. These consist of societies and associations which have been formed for social or professional reasons. This includes clubs, schools, women's organizations, youth centers, and many other organizations. The distribution of films to these self-equipped groups is a relatively easy matter, and the usual way of reaching them is through the film libraries.

Invited Audiences. These may consist of half a dozen company directors, members of the press, or specific invited groups. For example, films are sometimes shown to stockholders to give them an idea of the company's activities.

MAKING THE FILM

In making a film it is wise to use the services of an established film company unless specialist knowledge is available within one's own organization. It is possible to make good films oneself, using free-lance producers and cameramen, and it works out much cheaper; but this is a course to be adopted with caution. In general, one gets the film one pays for, and too parsimonious a film budget will be reflected in the result.

Established film companies charge considerably more than some private producers, but the sponsor can usually expect a much higher standard of production if he deals with a well-established company, fully equipped and employing a regular staff of high-grade technicians.

It is important to choose a producer with whom the sponsor will be able to work harmoniously and who inspires confidence.

The most valuable guide to the ability of a producer is to see some of his recent films. A producer should be pleased to arrange such a show, and it will permit an assessment of the technical standard of the films and give an idea of the producer's method of tackling different subjects. The producer should also be willing to give some idea of the cost of the films shown. This will provide an approximate idea of the likely cost of the film in prospect.

The production team—in order of their appearance on the scene— will consist of the producer, writer, director, cameraman, and editor.

This is the creative team, but behind them come the laboratory processing facilities and the recording technicians staffing the studio.

The Producer

The producer will conduct most of the preliminary negotiations with the sponsor. His or her duty is to conceive the way in which the sponsor's objectives can be achieved through the medium of film, and to interpret this to the creative team. Every film bears the clear imprint of its producer, and he or she is responsible for the production of the film and the selection of the team working on it. A producer, however, may have several films in production at the same time, and so it is important to have skilled directors and cameramen who can deal with the actual shooting of the film.

The Writer

The writer's job is to prepare an outline that is the working draft giving a general description of the film. The writer, or possibly another person commissioned by the producer specifically to deal with a very specialized subject, also writes the completed script—or shooting script—which gives the dialogue or commentary of the film and the shots appropriate to the text. The producer also sometimes writes the script, but more often prefers to be able to criticize the film objectively and so takes no part in the writing or direction. The writer will work closely with the producer at all stages of production, and accompanies him or her during the "investigation," when the producer makes the preliminary study of the subject of the film.

The Director

The shooting script is interpreted in film form by the director. In certain cases he or she may have written the shooting script. Directors are often particularly good at certain types of film, and it is the producer's responsibility to select a director who is suited both technically and temperamentally to the film in question. A good director is a skilled and highly paid person, for a complete knowledge of all the camera techniques available and the artistry to present picture and sound to achieve the maximum effect from the script are required.

Cameramen

In making a major film, both a lighting cameraman and a camera operator are required. The lighting cameraman creates a picture in light and shade by the siting of the camera in relation to the lighting: The success of the visual element of the film will depend largely upon this skill. The camera operator operates the camera and is responsible for the techniques that record the picture successfully on film. In many instances, the lighting cameraman does both jobs with the aid of an assistant.

The Editor

The editor's job is a most important one, for by cutting and arrangement a number of isolated sequences become a finished film. This is not a mechanical task; for example, it is the editor's job to evaluate the emphasis to be given to each shot by regulating the length of time it appears on the screen. The editor must work closely with the producer in order to achieve the desired result from the film.

THE SEQUENCE OF OPERATIONS

Once a producer has been chosen, it is necessary to furnish him or her with a statement of the policy on the film, which is known as a brief. The brief will normally include information on the following:

1. *The Objective of the Film.* This should state clearly what the film is to achieve. This statement will be the producer's main guide throughout subsequent work on the film.
2. *Audience.* It is important that the producer be informed of the audiences for which the film is intended and any particular characteristics.
3. *Content.* This should list all the material which it is hoped can be included in the film. The relative importance of the items should be given to the producer and editor as a guide to the intended emphasis of the film.
4. *Length.* This must be stated, but it will be influenced by the cost of the film.
5. *Facilities.* Details should be given of the facilities that will be available during the production of the film. These may include library information, use of employees and facilities, and so on.
6. *Time Factor.* It is desirable to state the date when the finished film is required.
7. *Distribution.* The producer needs to know the methods of distribution by which it is planned to reach the principal audience. This will help in determining the techniques he or she should use in making the film.
8. *Cost.* It is necessary to give the producer some idea of the amount of money available in order that he or she may suggest the appropriate type of film that can be made within the budget. In arriving at these figures it is necessary to allot sufficient money to cover the costs of distribution.
9. *Contacts.* The contact between producer and sponsor will normally

be through the public relations staff. It may be desirable in certain cases, however, to appoint a special liaison officer who will be able to ensure that the producer and film director will receive full cooperation and all the facilities they may need.

The producer will study the complete brief and then present proposals for making the film. Full discussion should occur at this time, as this is the best time to make certain that the producer has the right idea of what the sponsor wants to achieve from the film.

The next stage is the investigation. This is the period of study by the producer and the writer in which they assimilate the necessary knowledge and background to plan the film. They visit any facilities to be filmed and meet the people involved, working in close cooperation with the liaison officer (and the technical adviser, when required). Following the investigation, the writer prepares an outline of the film. This is the written presentation of the film, presented in such a way as to give a clear picture of the proposed shape and contents. The presentation of the outline is the first approval stage, and all members of the sponsor's organization who will have to approve the film should study the proposed outline, criticizing it on its general approach, content, and method of presentation.

The producer should now be able to give a fairly accurate indication of the cost of making the proposed film, and the sponsor can be provided with the first real indication of the ultimate cost. At this stage it is possible to cancel the film by paying a previously agreed upon fee for the investigation and proposed script outline.

If agreement is reached to proceed, the next step is the preparation of the shooting script. A number of technical issues must also be determined, such as the use of color, music, and commentary or dialogue.

The shooting script is the blueprint of the film. It is prepared in two columns. On one side of a page the visuals are described shot by shot, and in the other column the appropriate sounds (words, music, effects, and so on) are spelled out opposite the visual shots to which they apply. This is a very detailed document and will form the basis for the contract that will cover the making of the film. It is essential that this shooting script be scrutinized very closely and any queries discussed with the producer.

When the shooting script is received, it should be accompanied by a firm quotation for the production of the film with details of how the cost figures were determined. This quotation will be covered by contract, and provided there are no major alterations at a later date this should be the final cost of the film. When the contract is signed, the costs of investigation, treatment, and script writing are normally included within the total price of the film.

SHOOTING THE FILM

If no extended traveling is involved, the actual shooting of a typical public relations film may take between three weeks and two months. In order to work efficiently, preplanning is necessary, as the camera team will not shoot the film in the order of the shooting script, but in the most convenient and economical manner. For example, all the shots in a particular location will be taken on one visit, if possible. On outdoor locations the weather can be a hindrance.

Still photographs should also be taken during shooting for later use for publicity purposes. Enlarged prints from the actual 16-mm or 35-mm film are seldom entirely satisfactory.

The Rough Cut

When the shooting as set out in the shooting script has been completed, the editor arranges the various shots in their correct sequence as envisaged by the script and produces what is known as the rough cut. This is the first version of the film, and visually it is fairly rough. The visual tricks—called opticals—which are used to transport the viewer from one scene to the next, are not inserted. The commentary has not been recorded, and the rough cut is thus projected silent. It may also be shown in black and white, but when a color film is being made some pilot color shots are usually included.

This is the most important approval stage. The sponsor can suggest the deletion of scenes, or the alteration of the length of shots where it is considered advisable in order to influence the emphasis of the film. Any basic alterations or new scenes demanded at this stage will probably be the cause of extra cost, but this should not be a factor if any rethinking is essential. When the rough cut has been agreed upon, the length of the commentary or dialogue can be considered, and the screening time of the visuals increased if necessary to accommodate the commentary. It is a poor film, however, that relies too heavily on the commentary.

The Fine Cut

When the rough cut has been approved, the editor and other technical staff proceed to the preparation of the fine cut. Opticals are added, and the film can be shown in its final form for approval. The music, sound effects, and commentary are now recorded, and the picture and sound tracks are married. The show prints can be made and the film is complete.

COUNTING THE COST

Filmmaking should not be entered into lightly, for it is bound to be a costly operation. It is, however, a very effective medium of public relations when the subject lends itself to film treatment and distribution can be organized successfully.

There are no fixed prices in the film industry, and it is thus difficult to form any accurate idea of costs before the script outline has been prepared by the writer. This is because in the cost of making films, the labor component varies from about 50 percent of the total in live action films, to about 80 percent of the total cost in cartoons or animated films.

Film producers who have a long series of successful films to their credit will naturally charge more than beginners, but whoever makes the film, there are always certain fixed factors that govern the overall cost.

Color or Black and White

A film made in color will probably cost about 20 percent more than the same film shot in monochrome. It is therefore important to consider carefully whether the use of color is justified. Most public relations films should be made in color for best results, but there are a few exceptions to this general rule. For example, if the film deals mainly with machinery, color may be unimportant compared with the function of the machines, and in some cases the use of color may actually reduce the dramatic effect. Another instance is when it is necessary to include library material that is only obtainable in black and white. Each case should be considered on its merits, and due regard should be given to the advice of the producer.

The choice of color process links up with the question of film size. All films shown in public cinemas are on 35-mm stock, whether they are color or black and white, sound or silent; but in most cases nontheatrical audiences require 16-mm stock. Thirty-five millimeter stock is more expensive, but a film shot on 35-mm stock can be reduced optically to 16-mm, the extra cost often being justified by the quality of the final result. Moreover, in this way 16-mm and 35-mm copies of the film can be used as the distribution requirements demand.

Where the budget permits, most producers will advise that the film should be made on 35-mm. Certain optical effects can be used which are not practicable in 16-mm. Protection of the original film can be effected by the preparation of duplicate negative and, where the number of required release copies justifies it, both 35-mm and 16-mm prints can readily be made by a dye transfer process. The result is a good-quality film with a first-class sound track.

The use of a 16-mm reversal film also permits the production of a good-quality film with a first-class sound track. As with other 16-mm reversal processes, however, it is a little less flexible in production than 35-mm. Optical effects are generally limited to fades and dissolves, and though protection for the original film can be effected by the preparation of intermediate negatives, the best results are normally obtained when release prints are made from the originals. Furthermore, enlargement to 35-mm is not recommended; if 35-mm prints are likely to be required, the production should be in 35-mm in the first place. Technical dye transfer prints can be made, though again it is preferable to use 35-mm originals for this purpose.

The choice of color film in any particular case depends on a careful assessment of all the factors involved, including the potential number of copies required, the cost of these in relation to the cost of production, whether or not 35-mm release is contemplated, the complexity of the effects required, and so on. Each case must be considered on its merits.

Sound

Few films can be made without the use of synchronous sound, but it does add considerably to the cost of production. If the sound is to be shot on location, a sound-recording crew and equipment have to be taken to the site; and if it is shot in studios, this involves the usual studio costs. It is often difficult to get amateurs to speak convincingly even when they are talking about their own jobs, and it is often necessary to use trained actors.

In making public relations films recorded music is generally used. If the film relies on its musical accompaniment to a marked degree, however, it is well worth considering the commissioning of a specially composed musical score. This will again add to the cost, but where the type of film merits it the money is well spent.

If the film is to include a commentary, this is recorded when the film has been completed and is dubbed on to the sound track. The costs involved are moderate. If a film with a commentary is intended for distribution in non-English-speaking countries, this should be made known to the producer from the outset. Foreign language prints will have to be made, and the film will be made with two sound tracks—one carrying music and effects, and the other the commentary. However, if the producer was not told beforehand, music, effects, and commentary may all be printed on the same track; if a foreign language version is then required, the music and effects will have to be recorded again, thus involving unnecessary extra expense. Another point which has to be watched is that some foreign language commentaries may require more screen time than the original English version.

The importance of careful preplanning is emphasized by the fact that when sound and picture are finally married, sound is printed many frames ahead of the appropriate picture; if an alteration in the film is demanded at a late stage, the taking out of a length of film and the insertion of a new shot thus becomes a difficult and costly change.

Animation

Certain types of films are more effective if they are made partly or wholly in the medium of cartoons or puppets, but the process is very expensive. This medium is very effective for dealing with detailed explanations of technical processes, and it is also used to get over the difficulty of language or for conveying abstract ideas.

In technical films, diagrammatic work may be better than straight visuals and much cheaper than cartoon. For animation there is thus a choice between cartoons, puppets, or diagrammatic treatment. These techniques, however, may add considerably to the cost of the film.

Lighting

Lighting is another cost variable. If the shooting takes place in a producer's studio, the cost of lighting may be small. If, however, electricians and lamps must be hired and transported to several locations, the cost may be considerable.

Location

It is naturally more economical to shoot the complete film in one central place, but the subject may demand shooting in a number of different locations. This may involve a substantial additional cost for traveling and subsistence.

Cost of Film Copies

The provision of additional release copies of a film is not a very expensive item. Charges vary a little between the different film-printing laboratories, and very much according to the number of prints ordered at one time. It is a good plan to order the copies through the film production company, as they will usually examine each print from the laboratory to ensure that the print conforms to the quality of the original acceptance print. A small charge is made for this, and there is also a charge for supplying the spool and the can, and a charge for Poly-waxing, if required. This is a protective covering process which considerably increases the life of the print.

The number of copies desired should be determined in advance to prevent unnecessary delay. Extra copies are advisable in achieving the widest possible exposure.

DISTRIBUTING FILMS AT HOME AND OVERSEAS

The distribution of the film to theatrical and nontheatrical audiences must be tackled in different ways.

Theatrical Audiences

If the film is made with the intention of distributing it to cinema audiences, arrangements should be made for the producer to negotiate with the film distributor industry.

To get a film shown on television, the sponsor or the producer must contact the commercial television contractors or the national educational television representatives. A film must be extremely good or must deal with matters of national importance to stand much chance of securing TV showing.

Nontheatrical Audiences

The distribution of films to nontheatrical audiences is more complicated. It depends on whether the audiences concerned have projection equipment, and on whether they are invited or existing audiences.

Existing audiences that have equipment are the easiest to reach, and are usually contacted through film libraries. Copies of the film are deposited in the film library, and details of the film are included in the library's catalog. The film is supplied by the library on request, and a small charge is made each time to the owner of the film. The main disadvantage of this method is that the distribution of the film depends on requests from borrowers. The owner of the film may, therefore, take steps to advertise the availability of the film; this is usually desirable. Another system is that in which the film library guarantees a set number of showings for an agreed cost, and the distribution will then depend on the money available. Most film libraries offer facilities for the repair and maintenance of the film and keep careful records of its bookings, the type of audience, and the numbers attending.

It is more difficult to contact existing audiences that do not have equipment, but there are various ways in which this can be done. In many instances organizations meet in such places as church halls or club premises which are suitable for showing films, and it is thus a matter of supplying the necessary projection equipment and the operator. This may be done directly or by using an agent who specializes in mobile film projection. The mobile film unit includes all necessary equipment and the operator; and the cost is quite modest unless the unit has to travel to some remote spot to give the show.

Public relations films are sometimes suitable for the existing audiences found at public events or wherever people gather together in the open air. For this purpose a special mobile film unit is required— one capable of showing films in the daylight and of giving film shows without dependence on power supply.

The most profitable way of showing films is to arrange special showings for an invited audience. In this way it is possible to control the choice of those who are to see the film, and it may be supported by a speech about the film or about the organization that made it. Suitable hospitality can also be arranged prior to the film or after it.

The object of such a special film show to an invited audience is to impress them or to influence them in some particular way. It is therefore desirable to ensure that the conditions under which the film is shown are as satisfactory as possible. There is no comparison between a film seen in 35-mm in a cinema and the same film seen in 16-mm in a church hall. Fortunately there are many small private cinemas which can be hired by the hour in most large cities, and it is usually possible to hire commercial cinemas in the mornings.

Overseas Distribution

Public relations films are often suitable for wide distribution overseas. This can be achieved by the sponsor's own overseas reprseentatives or agents, by selling copies to overseas film libraries, or with government help.

Publicizing the Film

Shows will be either to invited audiences or in response to applications from interested parties; it is therefore desirable to secure as much publicity for the film as possible. Details of the film should be sent to trade associations likely to be interested in the subject of the film, and to the appropriate trade and technical press. Some newspapers and specialized magazines regularly review new public relations and industrial films, and it is usually well worth arranging a special showing of the film for the press.

USING FILMS AT EXHIBITIONS

Films can reach a specialized audience at exhibitions. Exhibitors can show their films as a part of their exhibit or can acquire a suitable room elsewhere on the exhibition premises.

When exhibitors show films as a part of their exhibit, it may be in order to have an eye-catching focus of interest or to tell a story that is not easy to portray with other exhibition display techniques. A number of visitors to the exhibit can be addressed more efficiently and expeditiously by a film than could be done individually by the exhibit staff. It is also possible to offer the commentary in a number of different languages to the audience by using earphones.

Two methods can be used in showing films as a part of an exhibit: either by the provision of a small auditorium area within the exhibit— preferably with suitable seating—or by the use of an endless film loop projected automatically and continuously from a special self-contained unit. Both these methods use rear-screen projection. The picture is thrown on the back of a translucent screen and viewed from the front, thus leaving the viewing area unencumbered by the projection equipment. Naturally, only small audiences can be reached by these methods, and the sound level must be kept low enough to avoid interference with normal conversation on other parts of the exhibit or neighboring exhibits.

If films are to be shown elsewhere in the exhibition, it is advisable to assure that the equipment is satisfactory. It is desirable to have fixed times of showing and to publicize these adequately at the exhibit site. A ticket system may also be desirable in order to avoid overcrowding and possible disappointment to visitors. The acoustics of the room may mar the shows. Some of the spare rooms at exhibition halls are completely bare, and are so resonant that recorded speech becomes difficult to follow.

At some exhibitions, the organizers arrange film shows as one of the attractions for visitors. The program is made up by the organizers from films available, and exhibitors are able to offer films for inclusion.

FILM STRIPS AND TALKIE STRIPS

Film strips provide a halfway house between color slides and the fully animated cinema film. Film strips are much cheaper to produce than films, but are able to provide greater continuity and cohesion than slides and thus can be extremely useful in certain clearly defined fields.

Film strips usually consist of a series of still pictures photographed on a strip of 35-mm film. They can be used merely as a series of pictures projected in predetermined order to illustrate a live lecture, or they can be used in conjunction with recorded sound.

The advantages of using recorded sound as opposed to a live lecturer are twofold. First, the method of telling the story can be standardized in the most effective form. Second, the whole range of recorded sound (e.g., music, dialogue, effects, etc.) can be used to dramatize the story.

The pictures are usually in color and can be actual photographs, cartoons, diagrams, or drawings. The pictures are changed at the predetermined points to correspond with the recorded sound, either manually in response to an audible signal or automatically by means of an inaudible signal recorded on the sound track.

Film strips with automatic sound accompaniment require skillful writing and direction if they are to be effective. They are especially useful when the purpose is to inform. They are in effect a form of illustrated lecture, one enhanced by the support of the full facilities of recorded sound.

8

Radio and Television

The electronic media have entered a period of accelerated change. Rapid development has resulted from the advancements made in photography, in computer and electronic technology, and in satellite transmission.

The result is instantaneous live transmission on a worldwide basis, access to information on a global scale, and technological advancement in receiving systems that are changing the way in which man acquires information.

Equipment will soon be available at increasingly lower cost that will permit a wide choice in the selection of and access to information and entertainment.

The rapid changes in technology are having a dramatic effect on the communications industries. Some of these effects are:

1. *Increased specialization on the part of all mass media.* Magazines, newspapers, radio, and television stations are beginning to recognize that survival is related to fulfilling the needs of specialized interest groups rather than the mass public. Therefore, in recent years the magazine industry has been revived through the introduction of hundreds of magazines designed to appeal to specific interest groups. Radio stations are appealing to specific age, economic, and interest groups; the stations recognize the importance of refocusing program format as change takes place in society. As an example, pop music stations changed to rock and roll stations in some cases, then to disco music, and later to country and western music. Many stations have narrowed their appeal with the intent of maintaining the support of a special interest group.

2. *Resistance to the change that is inevitable.* The technological change is having dramatic economic repercussions on the print and electronic media.

Television is experiencing the greatest upheaval. Cable television is offering viewers choices never before available. Satellite transmission is increasing the choices and complicating the industry market since stations or cable companies are no longer limited in their viewer range. In fact, new technology will soon permit direct transmission to a home receiver without the need for cable systems or proximity to a local station. The technological advances are changing advertising markets and threatening current procedures for determining advertising rates.

The newspaper industry is particularly concerned about its ability to adjust to the introduction of electronic delivery systems; lawsuits have already been initiated in an attempt to control access to electronically transmitted news and to block the admission of other industries such as the telephone industry from entering the home delivery of news and information market.

3. *The necessity of specialization and the need for continuing education.* An individual can no longer be a jack of all trades in communications. The public relations professional, in particular, must recognize the need for specialized staffs or counsel in working with the various media. The changes taking place in the electronic media make this especially true. The necessity of specialization does, however, permit a public relations practitioner or counseling firm to specialize in the electronic media field. Otherwise, the practitioner should develop a general knowledge of the electronic media but not hesitate to acquire specialized counsel when needed.

Continuing education for those specializing in the electronic media is essential due to the rapid technological change. It is important that public relations managers recognize the continuing educational need of staff members working in this area and that they keep themselves aware of the advancements and changes taking place.

COPING WITH THE CHANGES

Public relations practitioners can best cope with the changes taking place by clearly identifying the specific publics within a society that an organization needs to reach. When these publics have been identified and analyzed through research, then the radio and television stations that best reach the target audiences can be determined and used with effective result.

The practitioner's primary responsibility is to know his target audiences and to assure that the electronic media selected will reach those audiences. This requires a knowledge of a particular radio or television station's listeners or viewers as well as the listening and viewing habits of the station's audiences in relation to time periods and programming.

Effective public relations plans will utilize a full range of techniques using radio and television. This may include advertising, public service announcements, talk shows, special event activities with sufficient appeal to attract radio and television coverage, and hard news releases with sufficient interest to survive the competition for inclusion in newscasts.

The plans may be continual or they may concentrate coverage in carefully selected time periods, using a media blitz approach for audience saturation within a specific locality.

9

The Use
of the Spoken Word

The spoken word is the oldest means of communication between people, and it still remains a very powerful medium of public relations—despite the competition of the printed word. It is only necessary to think of the speeches of Churchill, Kennedy, and Hitler to realize the possibilities for good or evil influence on the part of a good orator.

SPEAKING IN PUBLIC

One of the occupational requirements of public life is to be asked to speak at public meetings, conferences, luncheons, or dinners. The preparation of speeches is often the task of the public relations department. This is common today in both government and corporate public relations. A short speech, delivered with feeling, will always carry more weight than a long address read carefully from a prepared script. Too many speeches are prepared for good readability afterward rather than for their effectiveness as they are being delivered

If a person lacks confidence in speaking, or if he or she speaks badly, great benefits can come from taking a course at one of the speech-training schools. It is not easy to suggest to a chief executive that he or she should take lessons in public speaking, but the attempt to achieve the desired result by indirect methods should be made. It can be suggested, for example, that since the executive will be required on occasion to speak on television, a rather nerve-racking ordeal, a certain amount of preparation is desirable. It is possible to mention that politicians take instructions on how to be at their best on television, despite their obvious familiarity with public speaking. Another method is to arrange for the speech to be taken down on a tape recorder or on videotape while it is rehearsed. The playback may convince the chief executive that he could benefit from some special guidance. There is no disgrace in needing advice on public speaking any more than there is in needing coaching for tennis or golf.

Contrary to popular belief, it is not necessary to start and end a speech with an anecdote, particularly if that anecdote is quite unrelated to the subject of the speech. A good story is sometimes worth telling, however, provided it is really funny and well told.

There is plenty of sense in the old saying that a good speech should be like a dress: long enough to cover the subject but short enough to be interesting; and in the advice given to the young person about to speak in public for the first time: Stand up, speak up, and shut up. Very often an excellent speech is spoiled by its being prolonged unnecessarily. Few speakers can hold the attention of their audience once they start to repeat themselves. Some people are good speakers but have irritating mannerisms, such as rocking backward and forward on their heels or blinking excessively. These mannerisms are usually a sign of nervousness, and the speaker is unaware of them; but once he or she knows, they can usually be avoided.

It is possible to help a speaker in a number of ways. For example, microphones should always be tested beforehand and adjusted for height as required. The lectern should be at a convenient position and fitted with a reading light if slides are to be shown. If a blackboard is to be used, it is helpful to have chalk and an eraser handy. These are obvious points, but they are often overlooked. It is also a help if someone can see that doors do not slam when people enter or leave while a speech is in progress. Lastly, it is encouraging for a speaker if the front rows are filled. Left to themselves, people will often fill side seats and the back rows, making a speaker feel isloated and the task of communicating more difficult.

MICROPHONE TECHNIQUE

It is strange that so many people have an aversion to speaking into a microphone. Even when one is provided, it is common to see a speaker push it aside and try to manage without it. If he or she has a naturally resonant and powerful voice, well and good; but so often the people who object to using a microphone are the very ones who need its help. A modern microphone, in any case, does not require one to speak *into* it, but merely *toward* it—and in an ordinary voice. Where there is a panel of speakers on a platform who remain seated while speaking, it is useful to have a microphone on the table in front of each speaker rather than one on a long stand, which is rather cumbersome under these conditions. A neck microphone is also very useful if a speaker is moving about.

A good speech can have a more lasting effect than any other single medium of public relations. It is therefore worth a considerable amount of effort to ensure that it is the right speech for the right occasion, delivered by the most able orator in his or her best manner and under the most propitious circumstances. This is the counsel of perfection which, if seldom achieved, is nevertheless well worth working toward.

THE VOICE OF THE FIRM

Telephone technique is often the Achilles' heel in an organization's relations with the outside world. Even in instances where meticulous attention is paid to every factor affecting the image of the firm, the telephone technique is often forgotten or ignored.

In many instances, the telephone operator or receptionist is the first member of an organization with whom an outside person makes contact, and the manner of the receptionist may play an important part in the first impression received—proverbially so important. The receptionist needs to sound courteous, alert, interested, and cheerful. He or she should convey courtesy, competence, efficiency, and friendliness. Proper telephone training will do much to establish a positive image for an organization.

Telephone receptionists should be given good conditions under which to work, and adequate arrangements should be made for relief by trained personnel during breaks, holidays, or sickness. It is equally important to ensure that there are sufficient incoming telephone lines and an adequate number of internal extensions. The need for good telephone manners applies throughout the organization, right up to the top.

It is the duty of public relations to see that the voice of the firm is courteous, but the work of daily supervision of the telephone is more appropriately the duty of the office or staff manager. The public relations director's responsibility is to assure that a telephone procedure exists that provides a courteous, responsive image and that it is being used.

There are occasions when some organizations receive such a rush of telephone inquiries that it is not humanly possible to answer each call immediately. The problem can be solved by using automatic answering equipment. There are many instances where the installation of equipment of this kind will help to avoid annoyance to telephone inquirers. It is also very useful for recording messages in the absence of the subscriber.

10

Advertising and Public Relations

Claim was made in Chapter 1 that advertising is logically a part of public relations since it affects relationships between an organization and the public, and that in the future it may become common for the person in charge of public relations to be responsible also for advertising. Whatever the case, there is undoubtedly a need for those in public relations to know how advertising works, and vice versa.

It is not proposed to examine here in detail the practice of advertising, since there are many good textbooks that deal with this subject, but there are a number of aspects of advertising that are of particular concern to those engaged in public relations and which thus merit attention here.

PRESTIGE ADVERTISING

Under modern conditions, it is not enough to make a good product, to market it, distribute it, and promote and sell it efficiently. Even a good product may not succeed if the policies of the manufacturer are weak or misunderstood by the public. It is necessary for a company to be a good member of society, and to let it be demonstrated to the public at large that it is playing a useful role in society. This is the reasoning behind the so-called prestige or institutional type of advertising, but it must also be borne in mind by those planning an advertising campaign.

Prestige advertising is probably the most difficult of all forms of advertising, which perhaps explains why so often it fails to make the most of its opportunities. There are two main types of prestige advertising. One sets out to tell the public of the massive contribution the company is making to the nation's welfare. The second type of prestige advertising is less direct in its approach, seeking to educate or inform on matters of public interest and merely including the name of the sponsoring company. One of the favorite subjects for this type of advertising is road safety, used very effectively by some of the oil companies and automobile manufacturers—and even by alcoholic beverage companies.

Before embarking on prestige advertising it is essential to define the objectives clearly and to know the specific audience it is hoped to reach. In some forms of prestige advertising the desired readership may be very small, such as a group of engineers or doctors or a select group of opinion leaders. The next step is to select the publications that will most effectively reach the intended audience.

EDITORIAL FEATURES

There are occasions when the interests of an organization are adversely affected by certain public misconceptions and it is necessary that the true facts should be presented quickly to the public. Under such circumstances the usual media of public relations might be too slow in their effect, and the answer is to take advertising space to publish the public relations announcement.

Many people believe that newspapers—and, to a lesser degree, periodicals—will not give publicity in their editorial columns to organizations that do not advertise. This is a strongly held belief, but so far as reputable papers are concerned it is without foundation. Editorial staffs work independently of advertising departments, and the criterion for the publishing of a news item or feature is whether or not it is news, not whether it pleases or displeases an advertiser.

In technical and trade journals the same general principle applies, but there is closer contact between editorial staff and advertisers. When special editorial features are planned, the manufacturers or suppliers concerned are often invited to take advertising in support of the feature, but this should not be a condition of the editorial mention.

In many countries, however, this division between news and advertising is blurred, and it is often necessary to pay for editorial mentions.

SUPPLEMENTS

It is a common practice for the press to plan special supplements dealing with such diverse subjects as an overseas country, an industry, or the opening of a local supermarket. The purpose of these supplements should be for the interest of readers, but too often it is only to attract additional advertising revenue. This is not true in every case, for often a paper is prompted to plan a supplement by a public relations approach.

Any proposal to publish a supplement must be considered on its merits, but in general supplements succeed better in their public relations aspect than in their advertising value. For this reason there is a growing resistance by advertisers, who resent particularly any pressure salesmanship designed to force them to take advertising contrary to their better judgment. Supplements are even less desirable when the editorial is keyed to the advertising. This type of unbalanced editorial reporting is detrimental to the best interests of the press, and all in public relations should be wary of supporting special press features and supplements except when they are satisfied that there is an honest intention to discuss the subject objectively and impartially.

ORGANIZATION OF ADVERTISING

Only in very rare instances will a public relations practitioner need to design or place advertising; usually he or she will work through an advertising department or through an advertising agency. The public relations practitioner, however, should cultivate a critical appreciation of advertising, become familiar with the methods and practice of advertising, and understand the way in which advertising is organized.

At least 90 percent of advertising is devoted to the sale of goods and services, and this has led to advertising agencies taking a specialized interest in such problems as marketing, merchandising, and market research. The designing and placing of an advertisement for a client is merely the end result of an advisory service calculated to aid the client in a wide range of problems associated with selling. In very large companies the advertisement director or manager will be competent to deal with much of this, using the agency mainly for the design and placing of advertising.

The public relations department or consultant should be competent to advise on the effectiveness or otherwise of particular types of advertising and should also have views on the type of advertising agency most suitable for different types of campaigns. It is a great pity that this advice is so seldom sought.

11

The Place of Research in Public Relations

Research is a vital part of public relations since feedback is an essential element of communication and a necessary component of a sound management decision process. Therefore, research technique, both formal and informal, must be continually utilized by public relations practitioners.

Informal research can include the feedback received from telephone calls, letters, and comments relayed to officers and public relations staff within an organization. Procedures should be developed to record and systematize responses so that a continual evaluation process is taking place within an organization.

Formal research requires greater expertise and is, of course, more costly but more reliable than informal feedback systems. Both should be in constant use within any competent public relations program.

Research techniques have become more sophisticated in recent years as more has been learned about effective procedures. There is a need, however, for the development of low-cost techniques that can provide reliable results within a short period of time. Greater progress will be made in this area once the public relations profession evolves to the point that public relations faculties with interdisciplinary backgrounds exist within colleges and universities.

One of the difficulties of conducting research in public relations is that public opinions and attitudes must be ascertained, and many factors can interfere with the acquisition of accurate information.

MOTIVATION RESEARCH,
OPINION AND PANEL RESEARCH

Public relations is essentially an art of persuasion, and in order to influence people it is obviously helpful to know as much as possible about the way in which people think and the manner in which they react to particular circumstances. Experience and intuition will provide an answer, but where it is desirable to obtain more factual or statistical data it is necessary to employ the techniques of motivation research, opinion research and market research which have been evolved to provide the answers to problems of this kind.

The use of research in public relations activities will depend on the nature and magnitude of the activities.

Motivation research concerns itself with the investigation of the way in which people react to given circumstances or conditions. This depends on psychology and on the environment and social pattern of their life. These factors all lend themselves to measurement, but it calls for expert skill; it is essential to seek expert help where motivation research is likely to be helpful in the preparation of a public relations program.

Opinion research techniques are much easier to understand, but the mathematical basis of sampling, the preparation of quotas, and the evaluation of results are again the province of experts. It is desirable, however, for all in public relations to know something of the way in which opinion surveys are carried out and their limitations.

A third method of investigating public opinon is by using the panel technique. A number of persons are asked to serve as a panel and to express their views on various questions which are put to them. The panel technique is particularly valuable for following changes in public opinion if the same panel is called together from time to time.

OBJECTIVES IN PUBLIC
OPINION RESEARCH

The success of public opinion surveys depends on the willing cooperation of those members of the public who are interviewed. Such cooperation is usually given, but if the same people are visited frequently it is likely that their cooperation will decline and may dry up. Since public opinion surveys have an important part to play in public life, their use should not be abused. On occasion opinion surveys have been taken merely to provide an opportunity of holding a press conference to announce the results. Such surveys are undesirable, and have no place in public relations.

To be able to place any reliance on the results of an opinion survey, it is necessary to know the conditions under which it was carried out and the method of interpretation. The presentation of the results of an opinion survey should include details of the sample, specimens of questionnaires used, an account of the interviewing procedures and conditions, and any special circumstances relating to the particular inquiry which might affect the results.

SELECTING THE SAMPLE

The mathematical basis of sampling techniques is too well established to need discussion here. There are two ways of finding out the opinions of a group: either one can interview every member of the group, or a sample can be chosen that is representative of the whole group. Provided the sample is chosen correctly, the results obtained from interviewing the small sample will be similar to those that would have been obtained from interviewing the whole group—within a margin of error which can be calculated.

It is only very rarely that a census can be taken, that is, the opinion of every member of a group canvassed by post or by personal interview; and so almost all public opinion surveys rely on sampling.

There are two methods of selecting the sample. In a *random sample* the choice of those to be interviewed is made on a mathematical basis, and since every member of the group has the same chance of selection there can be much less likelihood of error than in *quota sampling*.

A very simple example of a random sample would be if the council of an association wished to ascertain the considered opinion of its members on a particular subject. The sample could be obtained by selecting, for example, every tenth name from the alphabetical list of members. The results of such an inquiry might be quite different from the majority view of those members who attend meetings of the association.

Another method of sampling the opinion of the members of this hypothetical association would be by the quota method, although this would be extremely difficult in this particular example. To prepare the "quota" sample it would be necessary to know something about the age groups represented in the association, their methods of practice, their income levels, and so on. With all these factors in mind, the researchers would prepare a sample calling for n members of each category to be interviewed. In the case under consideration random sampling would obviously be the easiest method; but in general random sampling is more expensive and slower to give results than quota sampling. Quota sampling is used most frequently in actual practice, for opinion surveys usually seek to obtain information about large groups of the population and not from closely knit groups, where random sampling would be simpler.

Quota sampling is not as accurate as random sampling, as it leaves much more to the judgment and integrity of the interviewer. An interviewer taking a random sample would knock at every tenth door in a street, returning repeatedly if necessary until a reply had been obtained in each case. A quota interviewer, on the other hand, would be looking for so many bachelors, so many single women, so many housewives with and without children of school age, and so forth. The interviewer has a considerable amount of freedom in obtaining the persons to be interviewed, and this makes it easier for him to falsify the results.

Considering the ease with which interviewers can falsify or distort results, it says much for their integrity that results have proved so accurate, particularly in view of the low rates of remuneration paid. In practice, the results of quota sampling have proved almost as reliable statistically as those obtained from random sampling.

The interviewer is the weak link in the chain, and great care is needed in the selection and training of interviewers and in checking their standards of performance. It is so easy for an interviewer to take refuge from inclement weather and to fill up the forms himself; or to help an inarticulate interviewee by putting the words into his or her mouth; or to go back time and again to houses where a friendly reception is assured.

SIZE OF THE SAMPLE

The size of a sample depends on the degree to which the results will be broken down into subgroups in the analysis. The more general the nature of the survey, the smaller will be the acceptable sample. Forecasts of election results are based on samples of between two thousand and three thousand, and the size is adequate for an inquiry into the views of adults on specific questions. The failure of opinion polls to give the correct result of elections is due not to the fallacy of the poll technique but to the intricacy of the problem. Supposing, however, the poll set out to ascertain the likely voting of the different age groups, men or women, those living in different parts of the country, and so on. This would require a much larger sample, probably of the order of 150 to 200 interviews in each subgroup.

Provided the size of the sample is sufficiently large to enable the results to be analyzed into the requisite subgroups, little is gained by making the sample larger. The accuracy of a sample is increased by making it larger, but only in the ratio of the square root of the increase. To halve the margin of error it is thus necessary to increase the size of the sample fourfold.

DRAWING UP A QUESTIONNAIRE

It is often said that it is possible to elicit any desired answer by framing the question in a particular way. It is also true that stupid questions usually get stupid answers. Many learned articles have been written on the problems of framing questions in a form that will stand the best chance of securing useful information in the replies. Drafting of the questionnaire is the most critical element of opinion research and its importance can not be overstressed.

When a trained researcher is investigating a particular problem, it is seldom necessary for a formal questionnaire to be employed, for the results of inquiry will usually take the form of a book or published report in which the methods of investigation used will be described in full. Where, however, an opinion poll is being conducted that will lend itself to a quantitative analysis, it is very seldom possible to work without a formal questionnaire.

Wherever possible, it is desirable to pretest a questionnaire. Such a pilot inquiry will determine whether the questions are readily understandable, and whether they are going to provide information on the points that are the main subject of the inquiry.

Apart from the need to avoid leading questions, it is necessary to frame the questions so that they deal with factors within the knowledge and mental ability of the persons interviewed. Seldom will a "yes" or "no" reply yield useful information, and the modern tendency is for the number of questions to be increased and for there to be adequate opportunity for the persons interviewed to explain their replies. Not all the questions asked will necessarily be related to the subject of the inquiry; some of them may be designed as a check on the reliability of the respondent or to give an indication of his or her personal views.

INTERPRETING THE RESULTS

When all the results of the inquiry have been received, it is necessary to tabulate them and to draw up the conclusion in such a form that they will yield useful guidance to those who have sponsored the work—and who will be paying for it.

The use of computers has speeded up calculations, which may be very complex even if the final result is a simple one. Without electronic methods, opinion research could not have reached its present stage of development.

When the results of the research are available, it is then necessary to consider what action—if any—should be taken. Presumably the expense of taking an opinion poll would not have been authorized unless there was a strong likelihood of the results providing the answer to current problems. Ideally, the public relations department of a large organization would be conducting opinion polls on a continuing basis, for it is desirable to know at all times what the public is thinking. The cost of a full-scale poll is so high, however, that it is likely to be employed in public relations only as an occasional tool.

As in other areas of public relations practice, there are great opportunities here for mutual assistance between those engaged in the field. When contemplating an opinion poll, it is worth considering whether other public relations organizations might have problems that lend themselves to investigation at the same time. By such sharing, the expense of opinion polls could be considerably reduced.

RESEARCH AS A BASIS FOR PLANNING A PUBLIC RELATIONS PROGRAM

Any public relations program must be based on a careful analysis of all relevant facts, and this will often involve a considerable amount of research. For this reason it is unrealistic to expect a public relations program to be prepared overnight, or for it to yield immediate results. This thought is behind the insistence that public relations should be deliberate, planned and sustained.

Research in public relations is not a separate subject; it is the very essence of successful public relations activity, since it collates the past and present experience of all concerned.

There is an urgent need for research into the results of public relations activity. We know too little about the effects of public attitudes on public action. It is desirable to be able to study the results of past public relations programs so as to benefit from their success or failure.

12

Conferences
and Hospitality

Conferences are one of the important tools of public relations. A conference is not a medium of mass communication, but its effect can be most profound.

ORGANIZATON OF CONFERENCES

Conferences are usually held to discuss policies or to debate matters of mutual interest, but their value lies as much in the opportunity they provide for people to meet and to get to know one another.

The organization of a conference—whether it be a large or small one—requires careful preparation and detailed execution. Regardless of the purpose of the conference, its arrangement is usually the responsibility of the public relations department.

The first requirement for success is to ensure that the conference location has audiovisual and other necessary facilities. There is no substitute for personal inspection, and a reconnaissance is essential before a decision is made on a conference location. Not only should the conference hall and the hotels be inspected, but also any places to be visited—including places where meals are to be arranged.

If a conference is to have an international attendance, simultaneous interpretation may be necessary and special food arrangements may need to be made.

Many printed items are required for a conference, and it is an excellent idea to adopt a symbol and a uniform style and color scheme. This simple device gives unity to all the arrangements. Apart from the obvious items, it is useful to print luggage labels and car stickers for the use of delegates. The symbols and style should be maintained throughout the arrangements, right up to the printing of the report of the proceedings.

The preliminary notice of the conference sent out to prospective delegates should give the fullest possible details of the arrangements in order to reduce unnecessary inquiry. However well the preliminary documentation is organized, there are always many formalities to be attended to when delegates arrive for registration, and great care should be taken to see that this takes place efficiently and speedily. The main essential is to have sufficient staff informed as to what has to be done, and doing it with charm and quiet efficiency. The registration desk should be open as late as possible on the night before the conference commences.

Special arrangements will need to be made to receive VIPs or other special guests, but it is equally desirable to see that *all* delegates receive a cordial welcome. Flowers, fruit, and cards of welcome in the bedrooms are items that make a deep impression, particularly when some of the delegates have come great distances.

Whatever the nature of the technical or business sessions, skill is needed to plan the program in such a way that ample time is allowed for delegates to meet together informally between sessions and during free periods.

Every endeavor should be made to keep rigidly to the timetable, and there should be sufficient staff to shepherd delegates quietly and unobtrusively, but firmly. A successful conference needs meticulous attention to detail, but all the organizing activity should be quiet and inconspicuous and not obvious to the delegates.

Invitations and arrangements should normally be made for the press as discussed in Chapter 3. Many conferences incorporate exhibitions or special displays, and it is usually possible to invite local residents to attend at restricted times. A conference, if it is large and well attended, makes a considerable impact on a city, and it is a good plan to let the local people know as much as possible about it, particularly when the subjects under discussion are of general public interest.

International conferences of a professional or technical nature have become commonplace; they provide an excellent opportunity for the interchange of ideas and the promotion of international understanding.

SOME THOUGHTS ON HOSPITALITY

The art of hospitality in business should be exactly the same as it is in private life. True hospitality does not seek to buy friendship; it is the background to the establishment of cordial and lasting relationships. Critics of public relations insinuate that it consists mainly of wining and dining and of entertaining lavishly to gain favor or to place other people under an obligation. This type of behavior does occur at times in the world of business, but it is definitely not a part of professional public relations practice.

The life of a senior public relations practitioner is a busy one, with the telephone ringing constantly and a multitude of details with which to deal. It is not easy to settle down to a serious discussion with a visitor in the office, and it is therefore convenient—and pleasant—to fix meetings at lunchtime, or over dinner in the evening, when it is possible to eat together and discuss matters quietly and without interruption.

One of the assets of a public relations practitioner is his or her contacts, and it is necessary to maintain contact with people by meeting them, having a drink together, inviting them to lunch occasionally, and taking the trouble to keep friendships alive.

In addition to having a good knowledge of the media of communication, it is desirable for those in public relations to be knowledgable about food and drink, the media of entertaining.

Although entertainment is only one small part of public relations, within the course of a year a public relations practitioner may be called upon to organize a wide variety of social functions and meetings. These may range from a full-scale conference banquet for five hundred participants, to a luncheon meeting for eight to twelve journalists, or even a dinner for four.

A luncheon or dinner party should be planned as carefully as any other operation, and all eventualities should be considered and allowed for. The arrangements should be flexible enough to cope with emergencies such as the principal guests arriving late or not arriving owing to last-minute illness, a major crisis, or other causes.

Even when a function is to be held at a first-class hotel or restaurant, it is essential to leave nothing to chance if the event is to be a complete success.

There are no firm rules to be followed in the choice of a menu. The important point is to ensure that the food is appropriate for the occasion, and that any known tastes of the chief guests are considered. Special provision should be made in advance if there are likely to be any guests who may have special religious rules about food. For example, it is wise not to include pork in a menu for a large gathering of possibly mixed religions.

Use your imagination when planning entertainment, and do not get into a rut. Large hotels are very similar in most cities, and visitors will probably prefer to visit restaurants with more local color.

An easy way of giving a meal an individual character when it is held in a public restaurant or hotel is by having special menus and place cards printed. If they are well designed, they are likely to be kept long after memories of the meal itself have faded.

The increase in the number of national and international conferences in recent years has led to a corresponding increase in the facilities available for meetings and catering in all major cities of the world. The result is keen competition to secure conferences and large meetings, and this provides much greater choice than in previous years.

III

PUBLIC RELATIONS IN ACTION

13

Finance and Industry, Trade and Professional Associations

Public relations in industry and commerce is a function of management. It contributes to the successful operation of a company or organization in proportion to the extent to which it is allowed to play its part. This fact has been accepted by most large companies, but many medium-sized companies have been slow to realize the advantages of organized public relations.

OBJECTIVES OF INDUSTRIAL PUBLIC RELATIONS

There are two main objectives of public relations in an industrial company. The first is to establish contact with three important sections of the public: its customers, its stockholders, and its employees. Securing the mutual understanding and cooperation of these three groups is essential to success. The second objective is to promote the company's services and products in a highly competitive world.

It is necessary to draw a distinction between a public relations attitude and public relations practice. Both are required in industry: The correct attitude toward public opinion should be present from top to bottom in an organization; the practice should be the responsibility of those trained in the art of communication.

In industrial public relations it is necessary to have a list of priorities in order that available money and manpower are deployed to maximum advantage. It is easy to be tempted into pursuing projects that would yield fruitful results; but there may be more important problems which should be tackled first. The order of priority will not necessarily remain constant, and will require periodic reassessment.

Some very effective public relations is being carried out in industry— both by companies with their own internal public relations departments and by others using consultants—but the general level of attainment is uneven. For example, one company is well organized for press relations and employee relations, but neglects other aspects. Another company devotes all its attention to community relations. The best results come from a properly coordinated plan based on a carefully chosen list of priorities.

AN ASSESSMENT

The importance of public relations to management decision making in industry was recently emphasized through the observation of the operation and function of a public relations department in a major United States corporation. The role the public is having on decisions made by top management in industry was readily evident in more than a dozen areas. Technical advancement in the communications field, creating an accessibility to information not available to previous generations, is one of the reasons for an increasing worldwide awareness and interest on the part of the public. An exploding world population straining water, land, forest, and mineral resources, however, is probably the main reason for the public interest in industry decisions.

Public awareness of the way in which industry decisions can affect the environment, conservation, national defense, and the economy has resulted in the public's realization that it has a stake in the decisions being made in industry; as the result, the public is demanding the right to know decisions and to be able to react to these decisions prior to implementation. Therefore, industry is finding that more and more management time must be spent in educating the public as to its problems and the reasons and justification for decisions.

Management in industry is also finding that it must know much more about the public and the various defined or specialized interest groups within the public which can have an impact on the industry concerned.

Public influence is exerted through the development of legislation; government regulation; legal system decisions; lobbying efforts of citizen and special interest groups; press coverage, editorial comment, and published letters to an editor or aired letters to a station manager; through the withdrawal of product purchasing support; and by public demonstration.

Industry management is rapidly learning that it is less costly to know the probable reaction of its publics to decisions so that courses of action can be planned in advance to educate and promote understanding. It is also learning to avoid decisions causing public reaction that will lead to increased legislation or regulation. Industry is learning that by ignoring or improperly evaluating public reaction, management decisions can be made which in the long range may be detrimental to the welfare of the industry.

Examples of some of the areas in which public opinion and concern are directly affecting management decisions in industry are as follows:

1. Energy conservation. The high use of energy by some industries is causing the industries to plan ahead to the inevitability of prioritization of energy use and the resulting justification for that use.

2. Conservation and preservation of natural resources. City, state, and federal legislation are increasingly controlling use of land, water, forests, oil, gas, and minerals. Industries are finding it more and more difficult to locate anywhere in the world without having an environmental impact. The fact that an environmental impact occurs due to the depletion of land, forest, minerals, and so on may result in an expression of public concern even when the location is thousands of miles away from the public expressing that concern.

3. National defense. The need for accessibility to and conservation of essential minerals, food, and water, and the need for strategic advancement in space and ocean technology are the areas in which public concern continues to focus in relation to national defense. The result of public pressures is the involvement and interaction of governments demanding access, encouraging industry development, or in prohibiting trade or development as a countermeasure to a political action. Either reaction can impact industry severely. The reactions are based increasingly on the attitudes of the publics concerned, that is trade embargos or agreements and the conditions placed on foreign investments.

4. Environmental protection. As technological advancements are made and as more is learned about the result of past technological advancement, the public is taking an increased interest in the preservation of the quality of life and of the long-range effects of those advancements on life of all types. Public concern today extends to land use and development; production processes, especially by-product elimination and storage; and even to the effect of the product on the environment—for example, the soft drink can, junked cars, and aerosol products.

5. Human rights. The advancement in the communications media technology can be expected to focus public attention on violations of human rights on a worldwide basis in coming years as never before. The inability of nations to absorb refugees will increase the concern for

violations of human rights. Industry is learning that development in countries where human rights are ignored is risky because of the potential instability of the country. Iran is a good example, as is South Africa. In the case of South Africa, some corporations have removed their investment when able to do so because of public sentiment. Others have dropped their plans for investment.

6. Equalization of employment opportunity. Legislation and government agency regulation establishing guidelines for recruitment and quotas for employment of minorities and women are evidence of public concern for equalization of employment opportunity. The number of women now working in jobs previously restricted to men is evidence of the responsiveness of industry to this public concern.

7. Health, safety, and welfare of employees. Judicial decisions favoring employees, government regulation, and extensive press coverage of violations are the ways in which public concern has been expressed for the welfare of employees. As a result, today's corporations have extensive safety programs with safety officers holding the status of vice-presidential rank.

8. Protection of investors. Protection of investors through compliance with reporting regulation is viewed as normal operational procedure today by industry; extensive steps are taken to keep investors, potential investors through analysts, and the business community informed as to management decisions and the corporation's financial condition.

9. Equitable tax structure. Public perceptions of industry tax structures are increasingly recognized as important to industry through their impact on political decisions, whether on the federal, state, or local level. Therefore, companies are more frequently communicating to their publics the tax support they are providing and how it benefits the individual taxpayer.

10. Reasonable profits. The importance of the public viewpoint as to what is a reasonable profit has been emphasized recently by profits reported by oil and telephone companies. The ramifications are political examination and additional regulation. Industry is finding it increasingly necessary to justify and educate the public as to the need for substantial profits in order to support technological advancement.

11. Quality control and safety of products and services. Never before has society been so demanding of consumer protection. Court decisions and federal regulation have made industry sensitive to public attitudes toward industry responsibility. Industry is testing products in every conceivable way and has learned that product recall does not tarnish the image of the industry when responsibility is demonstrated and when concern for the public welfare is conveyed.

12. Elimination of unnecessary and costly regulation. Industry has learned that by informing the public of regulation that has increased costs to the consumer, public support can be acquired for elimination of unnecessary regulation. It is also learning the value of communicating self-regulation.

13. Integrity of management. In recent years the public has demonstrated a direct interest in the way a corporation or company conducts its business—specifically, in the way it interacts with governments and political structures. The impact of this public concern is evident in the restrictions placed on political gifts, on the development of more stringent guidelines for lobbyists, and by the increased interest of the press in seeking information about corporate business relationships in other countries. As a result, corporations are developing ethical guidelines and standards for their executive officers to prevent legal action and embarrassing public exposure. As the result of public attitudes, companies are also evaluating business procedures within countries prior to investment and backing away from investment in countries where accepted business practice would compromise their integrity.

14. Right to information. The public's increased access to information on an instantaneous basis is resulting in an increased worldwide acceptance of the public's right to know information, particularly information relating to decisions or actions that will in some way affect a public.

Access to information in government and the procedures that have been implemented to permit public expression of agreement or disagreement with proposed decisions, regulation, or legislation in city, county, state, and federal government have helped create a public climate in which the right to know is taken for granted.

As a result, the failure to promptly disclose or provide access to information is viewed frequently with suspicion and interpreted as evidence of wrongdoing since there appears to be something to hide. This growing public attitude is one that industry must recognize and work within just as government has during the past decade.

CUSTOMER RELATIONS

Relations with customers depend very much on quality, price, and delivery times, but also very directly on the reputation of the company. Public relations can play a vital part in safeguarding a reputation or in building a new "public image." It can also improve methods of communication with existing and potential customers. *Communications* is used here in its widest sense—that is, embracing all the media described in Part II of this book.

STOCKHOLDER RELATIONS

In the past, the sending out of the annual accounts and balance sheets was often the only contact between a company and its stockholders. This annual report, which was usually a legal requirement, was often little more than a mass of figures and statistics. It is now common for public relations advice to be sought in the preparation of the report, in order that it may give as much information as possible to stockholders. The design and typography of annual reports have improved beyond all recognition within the past few years.

Companies can make other efforts to keep in touch with their stockholders—for example, by inviting them to film shows, or to open houses at factories, sending them copies of house journals, and so forth. The approach will depend on the nature of the company's business—for example, a shipping company may invite stockholders to visit new ships of the company's fleet.

This branch of public relations can yield good results. The winning of stockholders' sympathy and support can be invaluable in the face of unwanted takeover bids. It can facilitate the raising of further capital by rights issues, and generally strengthen the company's financial standing with the big institutions and with bankers, suppliers, and others.

The annual general meeting can be made a public relations occasion instead of the mere formality it so often is, and stockholders can be encouraged to attend by holding the meetings in cities where large numbers of stockholders reside. Alternatively, some meetings of the board can be held in locations other than where the company headquarters are located, followed by receptions for stockholders living in the locality. Anything that can bring stockholders into closer touch with the board will serve to strengthen the company.

EMPLOYEE RELATIONS

Internal public relations is an extremely wide field. It embraces almost everything—other than pay—that encourages employees to make their maximum contribution to productivity and the prosperity of the company. The field is not sharply defined; it overlaps with personnel welfare and safety, labor relations and education, and must work in harmony with these other equally important facets of industrial management.

Public relations can contribute to the creation of an atmosphere in which people will work more effectively and willingly, and therefore produce better products or services at lower costs; it can initiate suggestion schemes and safety campaigns; it can lessen waste and carelessness and absenteeism; and, perhaps most important of all, it can enable management to communicate more effectively with employees at all levels. The methods used will include house journals (see Chapter 4), joint-consultation techniques, and all the media of communications and information.

In many instances, employees of a company and their families represent a large proportion of a local population, and in such cases careful attention to community relations is essential. Under these circumstances, local press relations become very important.

Public relations cannot guarantee the prevention of strikes or establishment of labor unions, but a well-conceived public relations program can play a useful part in eliminating misunderstanding and lack of information, which often lead to industrial action.

AN AID TO RECRUITMENT

Very large sums of money are expended on advertising to attract young people and graduates into industry. Public relations can also play a major role in recruitment, for the reputation of a company is an important factor in attracting employees.

Personal contact, direct mail, and well-produced publications all have their place, but perhaps an even better idea is to try to persuade potential recruits to visit the company's facilities, to meet senior members of the staff, and even to take part in internship programs offered by the organization.

PUBLIC RELATIONS
IN SUPPORT OF SALES

The ultimate aim of most companies or organizations is to sell their products or services at home and overseas. The role of public relations in improving methods of communicating with existing and potential customers has already been mentioned, but there are many other ways in which public relations assists sales promotion.

Press relations is of prime importance, and this will include the financial press and the technical press in addition to the national and area newspapers. The trade and technical press, in particular, form a valuable ally in most forms of sales promotion. Trade press editors frequently need news for their editorial columns: news about new methods of production, new raw materials, sales campaigns, and news about personalities or business deals.

There are, in addition, special shopping features in most newspapers and periodicals, and reporters seek news of new fabrics, new gadgets, and reliable information on anything that will interest their readers.

It can be argued that product publicity is more akin to sales promotion than it is to public relations. Insofar as it relates to editorial publicity, however, it is usually conducted from the public relations department, although it may be handled by a separate subsection.

One development has been the proliferation of special weeks or months. A rather similar idea is the selection of beauty queens such as Maid of Cotton. Used with discretion, valuable results can be achieved from the holding of a special week or the crowning of a queen, but these are ideas that attract by their novelty and therefore should not be used indiscriminately.

Exhibitions, publications, posters, films, and advertising all play an important part in industrial public relations, and they have been discussed in earlier chapters.

LIAISON WITH SPECIALIZED GROUPS OF THE PRESS

The practice of press relations has been dealt with in detail in Chapter 3, but there is one aspect that has a particular importance in industry although it does also apply in some other fields. The tendency has been for journalists with like interests to band themselves into associations. These groups usually have an executive secretary who can give useful guidance on suitable dates for proposed facility visits, and in general express an opinion as to whether association members are likely to be interested in information on specific subjects.

Apart from these formal groups, there are many small groups of journalists or editors who form a natural circle of interest to different sections of industry. For example, the editors of the electrical engineering journals are often invited as a group to informal luncheons or meetings. These meetings are for the purpose of imparting background information and answering questions; they play a very useful part in press relations.

The head of a small company will find it beneficial to establish friendly relations with the editor of the local newspapers, who may well be the local correspondent of a wire service and is, therefore, a link with the outside world. The editor should be invited to look around the factory and to hear about future plans.

INDUSTRIAL PUBLIC RELATIONS WORLDWIDE

Many companies have worldwide interests, and it is desirable to supplement the public relations at headquarters by complementary arrangements in all the areas where the company has significant business interests.

This may be achieved by working through the company's foreign agents, by engaging the services of public relations consultants in the countries concerned, or by establishing foreign branch public relations offices.

The foreign agents are usually well informed on local conditions, and may have useful contacts with local press; but they often represent a number of different manufacturers, possibly from different countries. Even if the agent has the necessary knowledge and experience to promote effective public relations, it is unlikely that the time or staff will be available to accomplish it adequately.

If a company's activities in an area are substantial, or if there is a subsidiary company operating there, it is worth considering the establishment of a locally based public relations office. This provides a closer measure of control than any other method. The alternative is to employ public relations consultants, and this would be the method of choice if the operations in the particular area were not extensive or perhaps varied in intensity. This point is developed further in Chapter 17.

Whichever of the two latter methods is adopted, it is desirable that the persons carrying out public relations for the company should be brought to the headquarters in the initial stages and given a thorough briefing on the company and its products and services. The visit would also provide the opportunity for a refresher course on public relations practice as it is understood by the parent company. If personnel in several different parts of the world are concerned, it is a good plan to bring them all to headquarters at the same time for briefing, as this gives them an opportunity to meet one another and form a basis for future cooperation. The procedure would cost more than if the head of the public relations department visited the branches, but the beneficial effect of bringing them together for initiation and briefing is worth the additional expense. This can be followed up—say in eight to ten months' time—by visits to the branches.

WORKING WITH OTHERS
SHARING COMMON INTERESTS

In public relations there are many opportunities for cooperating with other organizations that share common spheres of interest. It is obviously sensible for makers of steel to cooperate with users, for oil companies to work with automobile manufacturers, for railroads to cooperate with large users of freight services, or for airlines to link with makers of aircraft, engines, and components. In the field of consumer goods and services there are even more opportunities for cooperation.

When two or more public relations departments are working together on a project, it is most desirable that there be a clear understanding on individual responsibility. For example, if a press conference is held, the arrangements should be the responsibility of one organization, with the other or others kept fully informed and cooperating to the full in accordance with an agreed plan. Failure to do this results in overlapping and confusion.

On large building projects, where there may be a number of main contractors involved, it is desirable that there be coordination of public relations. It is very confusing to the press if announcements about the project are issued by a press officer working for a firm supplying some very minor service.

There are many opportunities in public relations for working together with other practitioners, and one of the benefits of membership in the Public Relations Society of America or the International Public Relations Association is the chance to meet and to discuss mutual problems.

LIAISON WITH CONGRESS AND STATE LEGISLATURES

The importance of congressional or legislative liaison in industrial public relations varies according to the nature of an organization's interest. If legislation is desired, or feared, the education of lawmakers will be high on the list of priorities. In such cases, it will be wise to seek the help of an experienced lobbyist.

Personal contact is always the best way of establishing mutual respect, and many organizations invite congressional and legislative leaders to informal luncheons or dinner parties where matters of interest can be discussed off the record.

The life of an elected official is such a busy one that it is better for him or her to be approached by associations speaking for a number of companies than by every single firm. Every company, however—and indeed, every individual—has the right to discuss problems with their representatives.

Most effort, however, should be spent in educating and in developing rapport with congressional and legislative staffs. It is the staff members who will perform the research that will eventually determine political positions.

TRADE ASSOCIATIONS

The activities of a trade association cover a very wide field in serving its members, but at least 75 percent of its work falls within the field of public relations. It is often difficult to isolate the different aspects of an association of this kind, but a major part of its function is to create understanding and foster cooperation between its members, and to serve as a bridge between them and the outside world.

It is impossible to generalize about these associations, as they differ in purpose and size and in complexity of organization. All trade associations, however, practice public relations—some as part of their management, others through a separate department. In some instances a small association carries out an ambitious public relations program on behalf of its members, who provide the funding through dues. Most large associations have found it satisfactory to have their own internal public relations department, but a small association would find it more practical to employ an outside consultant. It is not possible for the association officers to maintain a sustained level of public relations activities in addition to their other manifold duties, and in most instances these senior executives lack the experience or the public relations outlook essential for success in this field.

The following are some of the public relations activities that are likely to be carried out by associations—

1. Acting as spokesman for the members, or their industry, and representing their interests on official and semi-official committees and in negotiations with government departments.
2. Carrying out statistical and other forms of research, and providing an information service for the press, for members, and for others interested in the industry.
3. Organizing collective displays, demonstrations, and exhibitions; and holding conferences and meetings.
4. Providing export information and giving advice on overseas markets.
5. Publishing journals, bulletins, reports, and so forth, both for the private use of members and for informing outside opinion on the activities of the industry.
6. Making films, or seeking other forms of publicity, to further the interests of the members of the association, for example, by encouraging new entrants to the industry.

It is usual to have as president of the association an individual recognized as an outstanding leader in the field who is willing to speak in public about the association's aims and objects. The public relations director, frequently the executive director, provides the president with necessary counsel and support.

The common belief is that trade associations exist to maintain high prices, and that their actions are mainly inimical to general public interest. This mistaken opinion springs from the failure of trade associations to explain their function more clearly to the public. Indeed, in many instances even members of an association have only a very vague idea of its activities.

In trade unions, also, there is often a general lack of appreciation of the importance of public relations, and many of the difficulties of the trade union movement have sprung from a failure to inform the public and to seek their approbation.

Members should keep in close touch with their trade association, which is the natural repository of an industry's latest information, achievements, and problems. And trade associations should keep their members informed as to their activities.

The Trade Association's Strength as a Public Relations Agency

Public relations carried out by a trade association on behalf of its members has an authority that is often lacking when done by individual companies, for the following reasons:

1. The association can speak for a whole industry and therefore with detachment, balance, and accuracy.
2. The views and help of trade associations are often sought by newspapers and broadcasting authorities, which might consider that the views of an individual company are more likely to be colored by self-interest.
3. A big trade association has the finance and resources to plan group activities for an industry, such as films, exhibitions, and so on.

PROFESSIONAL ASSOCIATIONS AND SCIENTIFIC BODIES

A professional association is composed of individuals as members, in contrast to a trade association, which usually has limited companies as its members. This difference induces a different emphasis, but in general all that has been said about the need for public relations in trade associations applies equally in the case of professional bodies. Often the need is greater, for professional men and women often appear to like secrecy for secrecy's sake when a more enlightened attitude would be to their own advantage. Any one who has carried out public relations activities for professional bodies can testify to the frustration engendered by this indifference to public opinion and by the ingrained desire for secrecy.

The same attitude prevails in scientific bodies, but with more justification. Scientific progress is usually a slow and continuing process, and premature disclosure of results—or wild claims—could be very embarrassing for all concerned. Even when new discoveries have been made, the scientists like to wait until time has shown the value of the new ideas beyond all doubt.

Nevertheless, science cannot prosper without the sympathy of public opinion, and many leading scientists have broken down the old barriers and have taken positive steps to keep the public informed on new developments. Radio and television have made a notable contribution in this respect.

This enlightenment is spreading slowly to scientific bodies in general, and there is a growing willingness to adopt public relations ideas in order to win the public understanding and goodwill which is so helpful to the achievement of their objectives. But there is still a need for scientific bodies to use modern methods of mass communication to inform the public of the meaning of scientific advances. There is an equally great need to attract the required numbers, and quality, of young men and women into scientific occupations.

14

Federal, State, or Central Government

Public relations is an essential part of management, and this is as true in federal government as in industry. The function of public relations in government is essentially nonpolitical. Political parties organize public relations to publicize or promote their party's policy and candidates. Public relations in a government department, however, has two main tasks: to give regular information on policy, plans, and achievements of the department; and to inform and educate the public on legislation, regulations, and all matters that affect the daily life of citizens. It must also advise both elected and appointed officials of reaction and potential reaction to actual or proposed policies.

The advantage of having an efficient public relations program in government has become generally accepted and is found today in most government departments. The duties of public relations divisions vary somewhat, and so do the names. For example, the terms *press secretary, head* or *director of information division, chief information officer,* and *public affairs officer* are all used.

In most segments of government, from the local to the national level, the public relations division has an opportunity to express an opinion in discussions at all levels, and the head of the division enjoys the full confidence of the senior officials of the department. It is recognized that the chief public relations officer cannot fulfill his or her duties without access to full information, and that he or she should be consulted when policy is being formulated.

Public relations in federal government has had an increasing role during the last decade. The many special interest groups that emerged during the 1960s and 1970s spurred the development of public relations in government. The activism of the special interest groups and their effectiveness in influencing congressmen as well as their effective use of the media to generate public awareness of their causes resulted in the need for improved government public relations. Public relations departments that explain government programs and benefits and the effect of proposed legislation or regulation, and carefully monitor public attitudes, are now being viewed as essential to the stability of a department and to sound decision making in which the views of all interested parties are determined prior to the final decision process.

The most visible public relations division in government in the United States is that operated by the President in the White House. The names of presidential press secretaries have been familiar to most United States citizens since the John F. Kennedy administration. The growth and importance of the repsonsibility has paralleled the development of the electronic media.

Unfortunately some government public relations units are limited by law to function only as information clearinghouses with media relations responsibilities. The orientation or limitation is unfortunate and not in the best interest of the public or of government since the vital research arm of the public relations function may be ignored. Lawmakers concerned about the abuse of public relations in government have in some cases restricted the development of effective public relations programs because of concerns for costs, unnecessary duplication, the potential for abuse on the part of some administrators as a method for achieving personal publicity, or as a vehicle to protect and perpetuate unneeded programs.

These concerns deserve legislative scrutiny and carefully developed guidelines designed to prevent abuse. Yet it must be recognized that government, perhaps more than any other area mentioned in this text, has a direct responsibility to the public—and that responsibility requires openness and access to information. In addition, government must remain responsive to the public it serves, and this responsiveness can only occur when the means for two-way communication are built into our government system.

The increasing recognition of the importance of the public relations function on the part of government administrators has in some cases resulted in the performance of public relations functions concealed under many titles and in many budgets. It must be recognized that the actual cost to the taxpayer is higher when inefficiency of operation and effectiveness exist rather than consolidated, coordinated, well-planned, effective public relations programs.

Most government public relations is organized into media relations, employee relations, public affairs, and educational publication divisions. But there is no uniformity of pattern. Sometimes government public relations is divided into press relations, electronic media relations, publicity services, and a research function. A discussion of this organizational approach follows.

Press Relations

Press relations forms a large part of the work of government public relations, and it is beset by many complications not generally found in press relations work. The press or news and information office supplies news and explanation to the newspapers, magazines, journals, and other government agencies.

The press office staff may need knowledge on how to deal with (1) debates or hearings in Congress; (2) documents such as reports, bills, and so on; (3) statements by cabinet officers and department or division heads; (4) response to questions from the press on the part of the President or congressmen.

Television and Broadcasting

The growing importance of television and broadcasting as information media has led to the setting up of a press and broadcasting section separate from the press office, which hitherto served both press and broadcasting. The functions of the two sections are essentially the same, but the different nature of the two media means that they require different facilities.

Publicity Services

The publicity section concerns itself mainly with films, posters, leaflets, press advertising and other paid-for material. It works in cooperation with other government departments and state governments. When a department has an important message that ought to reach people throughout the country, it may not be enough to make use of the free media of publicity. Paid-for publicity and advertising make it possible to repeat information that does not keep its news value once it has been announced, and enables the department to present its message in full and in its own way.

Intelligence and Briefing Services

The fourth section of the department is usually a research section which collects information about the department and its interests and feeds it to the press and publicity sections.

The point has already been made in Chapter 1 that public relations is the responsibility of everyone in an organization and is not the sole prerogative of the public relations staff. This is equally true in government service. Every civil servant has his own contacts with the public and with authorities; these contacts are able to give him evidence of what people are doing and saying. The public relations officer can supply supplementary intelligence, and it is an important part of his or her duties to keep the rest of his or her department promptly informed on what is appearing in the press and what is being said and shown on radio and television. The officer should do more than this: He or she should try to ensure that public relations thinking is allowed to play a part in shaping all policies for it is easier and more effective to govern a reasonably well-informed people.

The desirability of governing with the consent of the people concerned generally results in long and detailed discussions taking place with a wide variety of interested organizations and individuals before decisions are reached. The public relations officer will usually have had an opportunity to express an opinion on the wording of the policy and the timing of its release, and will, of course, have the main task of publicizing it.

Questions addressed to congressmen reflect public interest, as do the questions that the public send to newspaper and magazine editors. Congressmen and editors welcome help from public relations departments in replying to questions; in rendering this assistance, public relations staff are able to keep in touch with current public anxieties and misunderstandings.

THE FUTURE OF PUBLIC RELATIONS IN GOVERNMENT

The old arguments as to whether public relations officers are necessary in government departments rarely arise today. They have become an accepted part of the administrative machinery of government, serving successive changes in administration impartially to the best of their ability. In the past it was suggested—particularly in certain sections of the press—that it was wrong to have experienced public relations officers in government, for if they did their work well it redounded to the credit of a particular government official and a particular political party. Years of experience have drawn a sharp line, however, between official information and party propaganda, between the departmental occasion and the political platform.

Most government department heads give their public relations staff the opportunity to make a useful contribution to the work of the department at all levels, but in a few cases there is still a tendency to regard them merely as press and information officers. The most encouraging sign is that public relations staff in government are being paid well—evidence that there is a true realization of their valuable role in modern administration.

15

Local Government

People suddenly develop an interest in local affairs when controversies arise over things that directly affect them, especially their pocketbooks. Public utility increases, compulsory acquisition of land, street improvements, and zoning are but a few examples. The resultant outcry over such things calls attention to the need for better local public relations. Public relations, however, is not a fire brigade to be called in to douse a conflagration of public opinion; it is the means to inform and educate the electorate to play its proper part in local government.

Local government is a shared responsibility, requiring a working partnership between the citizens and elected or appointed officials. Public relations provides the most effective means of achieving this cooperation.

The main objective is to develop a greater civic consciousness and to encourage citizens to take an active interest in their local government. This manifests itself in a greater willingness to run for elected office and in a demand that local officials give citizens an account of their stewardship. Increased citizen interest in local government helps prevent rule by cliques—however well-intentioned—and aids elected officials in adopting a constructive attitude toward their responsibility.

FOUR MAIN OBJECTIVES OF PUBLIC RELATIONS IN LOCAL GOVERNMENT

There are four main objectives of public relations in local government:

1. To keep citizens informed of a council's or commission's policy and its day-by-day activities.

2. To give citizens an opportunity to express views on important new projects before final decisions are reached by elected officials.
3. To enlighten citizens on the way in which the system of local government works, and to inform them of their rights and responsibilities.
4. To promote a sense of civic pride.

There are a variety of reasons why elected officials have resisted the introduction of public relations in their areas. It is a traditional characteristic of local authorities to be suspicious of new ideas unless they save money. Some fear that public relations would amount to propaganda in support of the policies of the ruling majority, undertaken at public expense. A third objection is that many elected officials regard it as their prerogative to maintain liaison between the council and the citizens. Even when elected officials are reasonably favorably disposed toward public relations, they fear that it will prove too costly. The opposition does not come entirely from the elected representatives, for some appointed officials resent the introduction of public relations experts who might, they think, undermine their authority or, by stimulating criticism as well as interest, add to their difficulties.

It is not public relations that is resisted so strongly in local government, but rather organized public relations. This feeling springs from conviction that public relations needs neither men nor money; elected officials will naturally know the needs of their constituents. The facts are sufficient proof of the fallacy of this reasoning, honestly believed though it is. Indeed, the need for organized public relations is greater and more clearly established in government—both central and local—than in any other field, for democracy cannot flourish in the face of an uninformed electorate.

Elected officials cannot meet the need unaided. They find that the meetings of councils and committees take up much of their available time, and most of them have either a living to earn or a family to look after. Few elected officials are able to master completely the complexity of local government, let alone find time to pass on their knowledge to a large electorate.

HOW IT WORKS

The public relations section in local government is generally a small one, consisting of the public relations officer, one or more assistants, and clerical staff. The public relations officer usually reports to an appointed official. The officer attends council meetings and committee meetings that have a particular bearing on his or her work or activities at the time. It is customary for the public relations officer to have the right to attend all committee meetings; the ideal arrangement, however, is to have this right but to exercise it as seldom as possible, for too-frequent attendance at meetings is bound to interfere with the efficient execution of the many tasks that require attention.

Local authorities have a duty to keep their own staff informed, particularly on matters that may have a direct bearing on them. It is also very important that members of an authority should be provided with information on all relevant matters. In both of these vital spheres, an efficient public relations unit within an authority can provide a comprehensive information service.

The work in a large city council will be on a larger scale than in a small county or township council, but the principles and conditions of the work will be very similar. In both cases the public relations officer will attempt to work in close cooperation with the departmental heads.

The most important single aspect of public relations will always be the personal contact between the members and officers of a local authority and the citizens they serve. If a person visits a city hall or country courthouse with a problem and is received with indifference or discourtesy, no amount of subsequent publicity will eradicate the unfortunate impression made. The first objective of public relations in local government should be, therefore, to do everything possible to break down the barriers to friendly relations between officials and the public. All contacts—whether in person, by letter, or by telephone—should be made as easy and courteous as possible. Some councils have induction courses for new employees which include lectures on public relations.

When a citizen goes to a seat of local government, it should be easy to find the required service or department. The design of such buildings often makes it difficult to place the various departments in any logical sequence—which is all the more reason why adequate signposting is essential.

RELATIONS WITH PRESS, RADIO, AND TELEVISION

The principles and practice of press relations, as discussed in Chapter 3, apply in general to local government. The local press is easily the most effective means of communication between a council and citizens and, therefore, it is desirable that everything possible should be done to establish and maintain good relations with local editors and their staffs in order that local affairs shall be reported as fully and as objectively as possible. Many people scoff at local weekly newspapers, but their influence in local affairs is often far greater than that of daily newspapers.

The press obtains its news of local authority affairs mainly from the agenda and reports of councils and committees. One disadvantage of this arrangement is that all the council news tends to be concentrated into one period of each month. Enlightened councils, however, take steps to ensure a steady flow of news to the press.

When the press unearths an alleged scandal, the public relations officer should offer full facilities to the press to investigate the facts. If a scandal really exists, then it is the right to have it ventilated, as this will help to encourage the council to take the necessary corrective action. The press is the watchdog over the rights of the citizen, and by and large performs this duty with zeal and discretion.

Relations with radio and television may not be as continual as those with the press, but their impact is usually more forceful. There are a number of documentary programs on both radio and television that seek out controversial issues and try to analyze the causes and ventilate the problems. Sometimes these programs take a subject such as housing, education, or adolescents, which affect the country as a whole; on other occasions they investigate dissatisfaction in particular towns or districts. There is only one satisfactory way to deal with this matter, and that is by offering all possible facilities to the producers of the program and by trying to ensure that they see both sides of the question.

On the positive side, radio and television producers will always be interested to hear about any unusual or characteristic local activities which might form the basis of a feature program or news report. Some of these activities may not rate national interest, but may fit very well into regional programs.

RELATIONS WITH LOCAL RESIDENTS

There are many ways in which enlightened local authorities have established good relations with taxpayers and other local residents, and have been able to enlist their help in making local government work. Unfortunately, few authorities employ all these methods—and some use none of them.

Information Centers

Conditions constantly arise in which men and women need guidance on their rights or responsibilities in connection with a wide variety of aspects of local government. Many authorities operate information bureaus which deal with inquiries made in person, by letter, or on the telephone. Such information centers perform a vital social service as well as a public relations function, and every local authority should have a central point at which inquiries can be dealt with expeditiously, efficiently, and, when necessary, in privacy.

The Printed Word

Taxpayers should not be dependent upon the press for all their information about local government activities. In most aspects of modern life it is customary to make an annual report to members or stockholders, and this need applies equally to local government. Each authority should render an account of its stewardship—annually, quarterly, or even monthly—so that all taxpayers know about local developments that affect them. The issue of such civic reports takes place in some areas and has proved its worth. This does not interfere in any way with the function of the local press, and indeed, newspapers usually welcome bulletins as an additional means of information.

Corporate Image

Councils are always looking at costs, but the desire for economy should not be allowed to debase the standard of printed material issued by councils. Good typography and printing cost no more than bad design, and here there is scope for public relations officers to persuade their colleagues in local government of the desirability of maintaining the highest possible standard in print design. This also applies to posters, notice boards, signs, exhibitions, and so on. Each authority should adopt a suitable house style so that all the council's productions are readily identifiable. This helps to establish a corporate image for the authority, which aids overall efficiency.

Exhibitions

In local affairs, where the population is concentrated within a defined area, exhibitions are a very effective medium of public relations.

When there is reason to justify a major celebration, a large-scale civic exhibition can be considered. Small-scale exhibitions, however, can fill the continuing need for the imparting of information on many diverse subjects such as welfare, road safety, health, and education.

Small exhibitions need not be costly, but ingenuity should be exercised to make the standard of presentation as high as possible. It is also important to ensure variety in the design, so that if the exhibitions are in the local library, for example, one exhibition should be clearly distinguishable from the succeeding one.

Cooperation between departments is desirable since the initial cost is the major part of a small exhibition. By a sharing arrangement, a number of government divisions or offices can use an exhibition in turn.

Points of vantage such as notice boards outside public libraries or town halls can be used for the display of information, photographs, and posters, and can be a very effective means of communication with the public if used with imagination. Such notice boards need maintenance and regular cleaning.

OPINION LEADER FEEDBACK

Attendance at meetings of service clubs, local societies and organizations remains one of the most effective methods of maintaining contact with opinion leaders in an area. A public relations officer should consider it part of his or her duties to maintain the closest possible liaison with local bodies of all kinds in order to convey information as well as to provide feedback to decision makers. This direct link with local public opinion can be most valuable in avoiding misunderstanding and facilitating efficient government.

SUMMARY

The arena of local affairs provides an obvious place for the function of public relations in almost all its aspects. Where organized public relations has been allowed to show its full potential, the results have been acclaimed as very successful; where local suspicion or prejudice has prevented its operation, an important and worthwhile job remains to be done. The effective way is to appoint skilled public relations staff with the resources to meet the needs of the area. This is not enough in itself: Every member of a local council and its administration must be kept aware of the need to follow the principles of public relations and to build up mutual confidence.

No mention has been made in this chapter of holiday resort publicity or industrial development, which are sometimes included in the responsibilities of the public relations department. Where a public relations officer has duties in these fields, they should not be allowed to interfere with his primary task of making local government live in the mind of every citizen.

16

Public Relations in the Community, Voluntary Bodies, International Organizations

There are many public relations activities that affect the general well-being of the population and which are divorced from ordinary commercial implications. This communal aspect is the main link between the activities considered in this chapter.

In the United States every sphere of communal life has its public relations advisers: schools, universities, public libraries, the churches, the police, public utilities, and so on. In the United Kingdom the initial interest came mainly from government and industry, with the community slow to follow.

Community relations is a very broad subject. Many aspects of community relations have already been discussed in Chapters 13 and 15 dealing with the private business sector and wtih local government. The primary mission of community relations is to develop or maintain mutual understanding.

LAW ENFORCEMENT PUBLIC RELATIONS

During the late sixties and most of the seventies, police departments found themselves the focus of public attention in relation to treatment of minorities, civil rights and peace protesters, and youthful drug abusers. As a result, many law enforcement groups found it a necessity to establish citizen advisory groups and to appoint a public relations officer to work with the groups as well as with members of the news media. In simple terms, law enforcement groups found it essential for their continued public support to listen and be responsive to the concerns of citizen groups.

Another important function of the law enforcement public relations officer is to sensitize other officers as to the importance of public relations and to educate them in techniques applicable to their everyday work situation.

MEDICAL PUBLIC RELATIONS

Medical public relations has exploded as a professional area in recent years, and thousands of new job opportunities in public relations are predicted. The fact that people are living longer, coupled with the now-aging baby boom which followed WWII, are the reasons for the growth in medical facilities and resulting new jobs. The revolutionary break-throughs occurring in medical knowledge and technology, combined with the skyrocketing cost of medical services, has resulted in new public demands. Justification for high costs and the desire for personalized attention from medical practitioners whose specialization and heavy work loads have removed them from family contact and the family confidence are two factors relating to the growth of public relations in the medical field.

Fund raising is an important part of medical public relations, along with the special event planning necessary to raise funds and to express appreciation to those who have contributed.

RELIGIOUS ORGANIZATIONS PUBLIC RELATIONS

Church organizations have learned quickly the value of using the mass media to reach audiences and propagandize their doctrines.

Major church groups are now maintaining competent public relations staffs in charge of publications, publicity, and programming, fund raising, and special event activities. The increased sophistication is evident the quality of programming and publications now being produced and in publicity, promotion, and fund raising methods and materials.

Further evidence of the increasing awareness of the value of the media and of public relations procedures is the recent establishment of the Christian Broadcasting Network.

SAFEGUARDING THE ENVIRONMENT

The public judges organizations by the way in which they behave, in the same way that individuals form good or bad impressions of people with whom they come into contact. Most large organizations are aware of the need to preserve the environment, and the electricity and oil companies, for example, go to considerable lengths to try to make new buildings and exposed plant blend into the surrounding countryside and obtrude as little as possible into local life. Any new industrial project, however, may interfere with local amenities, and great care should be taken to avoid pollution of the environment in any way.

A problem arose, for instance, over United States air bases in Britain. Local residents naturally resented the bases, with their attendant noise and other disturbing elements. The American authorities, however, took steps in cooperation with Britain's Ministry of Defense to prevent trouble. Each base had a British community relations officer, employed by the Ministry, whose task was to bring British and American people together locally and to break down ill-informed prejudices.

INDUSTRY IN A LIVING COMMUNITY

A company with a large factory in a town is a source of wealth to it both directly as tax revenue and through salaries paid to employees, and indirectly by stimulating other enterprises. The company will, of course, need to recruit labor locally, and there are many other ways in which it can be of great community assistance.

The need to play a part in local community affairs is now generally accepted by industry, and this may take a number of forms. It is quite common for senior members of the firm to take an interest in local politics, and it is good policy to make it equally possible for workers to serve on local councils or boards.

A large company is usually in a position to give financial help to local charities and local projects such as youth clubs, athletic programs, and repertory theaters. In some cases, firms donate public parks, meeting halls, and the like. This kind of participation in local affairs does much to establish a company as a good neighbor and a desirable employer. Where a high proportion of the local people work for a company, it is obviously desirable for that company to support local activities generously; but this is equally well worth a company's involvement when the labor force is comparatively small.

CONSUMERISM AND PROTESTS

The United States experienced the first stirrings of consumerism—the recognition that the interests of the consumer were of major importance. This movement has spread to Europe and many other parts of the world. Side by side with the growth of interest in consumerism has been a considerable increase in protests.

It has become fashionable for individuals or groups, aggrieved by events or proposed developments, to organize themselves in order to protest as effectively as possible. Their protests range from quite peaceful manifestations to sometimes violent eruptions.

The main difference between protests and professional public relations practice is that protests are usually organized by amateurs—although sometimes with professional assistance—and are limited in time scale, while public relations practice is usually characterized by its continuing nature.

The enthusiasm engendered by the sense of grievance of those concerned gives considerable impetus to protests, and many such campaigns have succeeded in achieving their goals. However, a protest tends to be a volcano that erupts suddenly but may soon be forgotten unless it achieves positive results.

Protests exploit all the usual forms of public relations methods and cover all media. Political activity at local and/or national level is usually an essential element in a protest campign.

WELCOMING VISITORS

Military establishments have set a good example to industry in hosting visiting days, special tours, exhibits, demonstrations, and shows as ways of securing public interest and cooperation. The military learned long ago that one of the most effective ways of establishing good community relations was by opening the doors to their ships or military establishments as often as practicable.

A number of industrial companies in various fields have welcomed visitors to their factories for many years and have been well satisfied with the results. The practice of inviting organized parties has spread, and some companies will show any visitor around their factories even without prior appointment. Evening visits may be a good idea in certain cases, as they permit family participation.

In some industries, the entertaining of visitors tends to interfere with production, and for this reason such factories prefer to hold open houses each year to which employees can bring their relatives, and when local residents and other people likely to be interested can also visit.

It is important to make suitable arrangements to receive visitors: This entails not only the provision of trained guides, but also of amenities such as adequate rest rooms.

After a suitable welcome, parties should be split up into small groups, each under a guide. The guides should have received adequate training so that they carry out their duties satisfactorily. In addition to having extensive knowledge of a company and its processes, guides need a sense of loyalty to the organization—and positive measures should be taken to maintain their enthusiasm. Among ways of doing this are:

1. Promising that the best guides will be selected to guide VIP parties, and giving those guides an extra fee for this.
2. Holding discussion groups at which guides can meet factory managers and hear about new developments and company policy.
3. Sending guides occasionally to visit other factories as members of ordinary visiting parties, so that they can see how others do it or learn some of the things not to do.

It is usual to offer some refreshments to organized visiting parties; for morning visits coffee or tea and sweet rolls will probably be adequate, while in the afternoon soft drinks, sandwiches, or cake will be suitable. Refreshments are usually offered at the end of a conducted tour, but if a factory is in an isolated location and parties have traveled some distance, it may be preferable to serve refreshments first or as a break during the tour. Souvenirs may also be provided for visitors, even if it is only printed material about the organization.

VOLUNTARY OR NON-PROFIT ORGANIZATIONS

There are thousands of voluntary or non-profit organizations in the United States and United Kingdom, and most of them face the constant need to raise funds. But whereas in some instances this is the main object of the organization, in other cases the money is needed for the pursuance of social work, youth welfare, and other causes.

The running of a large voluntary organization of any kind is itself a continuing exercise in public relations. Since the majority of the workers —both at headquarters and in widely dispersed branches—are unpaid, it is necessary to maintain their interest at a high pitch by keeping them in sympathy with the aims of the organization and by retaining their confidence in headquarters' policy and efficiency. Assuming that the policy of the organization is right, this resolves itself mainly into a problem of communication.

The internal communications are usually in writing and by personal contact between the officials and the branches and the members. Without incurring undue expense, it is always possible to improve the house journal—or to start one—and to modernize circulars, publicity leaflets, letterheads, and so on. Personal contacts are even more important, and the guiding principle should be to make them as frequent as possible.

The public image of a voluntary organization is very important to its success both in attracting financial support and in securing the willing cooperation of voluntary workers. It is necessary to show clearly that the organization deserves support and that it is performing a function which the state cannot—or will not—perform adequately, and which is not being done by other bodies.

It is clear that voluntary organizations need expert public relations advice, since their efficiency can be improved by the adoption of appropriate techniques. While there are special occasions when public relations men and women should give voluntary help, in general voluntary bodies should be prepared to appoint experienced public relations officials to their headquarters staff or to use the services of consultants. Unfortunately, the committees of voluntary bodies often include a high proportion of men and women who have no practical business experience and who mistrust advertising or public relations. These people are inclined to resist any suggestion of spending money on anything as intangible as public relations. It is necessary, therefore, to explain how it can contribute to the success of the organization, and to show that public relations is as real as print, films, talks, and other accepted means of communication, which are, indeed, its very essence.

When the headquarters of a voluntary organization has adopted a progressive public relations program, the next step is to see that this policy is also implemented throughout the organization. Lectures on public relations should be given to local branches as opportunity permits, and committees encouraged to make someone responsible for liaison with the local press.

INTERNATIONAL ORGANIZATIONS

The activities of the United Nations Organization are primarily political, but there are many associated bodies such as UNESCO and the World Health Organization whose activities have a profound effect on world educational cooperation.

The success of any international project depends on the pursuance of correct public relations policies, for it is necessary to secure and maintain the support of peoples of varying cultural, religious, and political beliefs.

Public relations for an international organization presents similar problems to those met in other branches of the work, but the canvas is so much wider that policies and techniques have to be adjusted accordingly. The public relations staff will be recruited from different parts of the world to avoid any national bias, and this helps to overcome the main difficulty of planning to meet the requirements of different areas.

The main media of public relations used within this field are publications, press and films, and the holding of conferences, study groups, and so forth. Most international organizations are doing excellent work in these fields, but there is almost unlimited scope for extending the activties, limited in fact only by available finance.

17

Public Relations
in Support of Exports

In the same way that public relations can assist business at home, so it can aid exporters to enlarge the scope of their overseas marketing. Organized public relations will facilitate the establishment and maintenance of advantageous business relations, and can be used in direct support of all types of marketing effort.

THE NEED FOR PUBLIC RELATIONS
AND PUBLICITY OVERSEAS

The competition in all overseas markets is so fierce that it is not sufficient to be able to supply the right goods at the right price and to be able to give reasonably good delivery. Direct advertising has an important part to play in support of overseas sales campaigns, but its effect will be enhanced if public opinion in the territory concerned is being cultivated by organized public relations methods.

The aim of public relations programs directed at overseas targets is first to protect the general reputation of goods and services, and secondly to enhance the reputation of the goods supplied by a particular company or industry. It might appear that only the second of these objectives is the concern of individual exporters, but unless the general reputation of a country's goods and services stands high, it will be difficult for individual exporters to extend their overseas activities.

144

THE ADVANTAGES OF COOPERATION

Many trade associations do excellent public relations work overseas on behalf of their members, and this is a service that should be given high priority. Manufacturers should give these cooperative efforts their whole-hearted support, for through them excellent results can be achieved for relatively small per capita expenditure. Cooperative public relations programs demand little from the individual manufacturer except financial support, but the implementation by an individual exporter of overseas public relations needs much greater organization and the use of professional help. Chambers of commerce are also very active in this field.

LOCAL KNOWLEDGE IS ESSENTIAL

It is seldom possible for a national of one country to be fully familiar with the nuances of public opinion and the complexity of communication media in other countries, and this type of knowledge is the essential raw material on which a successful public relations campaign must be based. It will therefore be necessary in most instances to seek professional public relations assistance in the overseas territory concerned. Many experienced and reputable public relations organizations—some independent, and others affiliated to advertising agencies—have close links with similarly experienced public relations organizations in the major territories and industrial centers of the world. An advantage of using the services of one of the internationally linked groups is that a campaign can be directed from the home country but serviced by nationals in the overseas countries concerned.

The extent to which the various media of public relations will feature in any overseas campaign will depend on the particular territory and on the nature of the product or service to be exported. It is in assessing the existing conditions, advising on the choice of suitable media, and preparing and disseminating appropriate material that experienced public relations practitioners can assist exporters to secure the best results from the available resources. There is no substitute for personal reconnaissance visits to the area concerned.

Many major foreign newspapers and periodicals have representatives resident in many countries. It is obviously good policy to maintain contact with these foreign correspondents and to give them every opportunity for securing news to wire home.

The abundance of good trade and technical journals with important overseas circulation provide a useful medium of public relations—especially in the technical field. Where another country has its own technical press, however, this should be acknowledged when planning a campaign.

Radio and television have a powerful mass appeal, especially in the developing countries, and industrial films made with television in mind can achieve a wide showing on their screens.

SPEAKING IN THE RIGHT LANGUAGE

Even between countries supposedly speaking the same language, such as the United Kingdom and the United States, it is necessary to ascertain that the correct choice of words is made, both to ensure clarity of meaning and to avoid the possibility of giving offense. This problem of language becomes much greater when dealing with Latin America, the Soviet Union, Japan, and other countries where English is not universally understood. Even in countries where a very high proportion of the population speak and understand English (such as Holland and Denmark,) it is essential to use the local language in publicity activities. It is reported that certain types of consumer goods sell well in Western Europe through advertising in English and using packs printed in English. This is due presumably to a social appeal that does not usually have a similar effect in public relations activities designed to inform and persuade.

The necessity of using the appropriate language for publications, exhibition captions, press releases, and so on, is obvious; the difficulty comes in securing thoroughly satisfactory translations. It is not always possible to get the translation done in the country where it is to be used, as this may take too long, but it is wise to get the translation done by a national of the country concerned.

If the subject matter is of a technical or specialized nature, it is also necessary to make sure that the translator knows the subject exhaustively and is cognizant of new development. Most people can recall sad experiences when translations have been done by willing workers lacking the necessary technical background. Whenever time permits it is wise to send a copy of the translation for checking in the country concerned. It is usually easier to get it checked overseas than to obtain the actual translation there.

It is not possible to put too much emphasis on the need for accurate translations, as misspelling, bad grammar, and the use of obscure idiom create a very bad impression at the receiving end. There is an opportunity here for trade associations and bodies like chambers of commerce to help their members.

It is essential to learn something about local likes and dislikes and customs, and to respect rivalries between neighboring cities or regions.

One example is the keen rivalry in Australia between Sydney and Melbourne; and similar rivalry exists between many other cities.

Another example relates to regional and ethnic pride. An alcoholic beverage advertisement run recently in newspapers in the southwestern United States had to be withdrawn because it showed a sleeping Mexican beneath a large sombrero. The advertisement was viewed as insulting by Mexican Americans, who resented the stereotype. The designer, no doubt, viewed it as picturesque.

It is necessary also to learn and use the correct names of countries. Too many letters are still sent to Africa, South East Asia, and other parts of the world wrongly addressed, and this often causes great offense. Above all, it is essential to remember that airmail exists, and not to send important letters by surface mail.

OVERSEAS VISITS BY BUSINESSMEN

The companies that do well in exporting are usually those whose senior executives make frequent visits overseas. These visits are made primarily for business purposes, but if those concerned are willing to give talks to local societies, appear on radio and TV, and give interviews to the local press, their visits can benefit national prestige as well as foster the businessmen's own particular interests. The planning of talks, press conferences, and so forth, on the spot is very much a public relations matter, and specialist advice should be sought.

Departments of Commerce and Trade give financial assistance to approved outward and inward trade missions organized by nonprofit bodies such as trade associations or chambers of commerce. This has been most useful in encouraging a greater two-way flow of experts and buyers —which can be a major factor in promoting increased exports.

18

Case Histories

The study of case histories is a very effective way to acquire knowledge, particularly if the reports mention failures as well as successes. A book on the practice of public relations would not be complete unless it included a number of case histories from different fields.

The following examples have been collected with the aid of those concerned, and they are offered as some practical indication of how public relations works and how it can achieve useful results. The choice was restricte. by the fact that public relations is usually a confidential service. Many fascinating case histories that one hears about in confidence cannot be reported.

PUBLIC RELATIONS FOR THE POLICE

Britain's police operate on a basis of public cooperation, but traditionally the police attitude to the public in general, and the media in particular, has been essentially defensive.

However, in most police headquarters a distinct departure from this traditional stance is beginning to be seen and felt. It is possible that in certain areas individual police officers may soon be able to deal with the news media on their own initiative, and the question of training in TV technique for police officers is said to be under consideration.

New Scotland Yard has had its own public relations department since 1967. This consists of two branches, one dealing solely with press relations and the other with publicity. The News Branch, some twenty-five strong, includes the long-established press bureau, now modernized to provide a twenty-four-hour news service for getting accurate information to reporters and ensuring that the best contacts are available for interview.

In the United States, many law enforcement divisions now have an officer designated as the public relations officer. His or her responsibilities will include media relations as well as community relations. In addition to arranging press conferences and working with the press on a daily basis, the officer may also work with citizens groups appointed to aid the police in their relationship with minority groups and with community service organizations.

AERIAL AMBASSADOR

When Goodyear decided in 1972 to build a dirigible in the United Kingdom, it was a major decision that affected not only the company's airship history but also the whole history of British airship building. The helium-filled airship, which was christened *Europa,* was the first to be built in Britain for over twenty years.

The airship was fully equipped as a virtually static television transmitting platform, and in the summer of 1973 the BBC used it to televise the European Grand Prix motorcar race from Brands Hatch.

The *Europa* was a tremendous public relations asset. Wherever it went, its flight path was well covered by journalists and newspaper photographers, and Goodyear arranged for many members of the press to fly in it.

A good example of the way the project was handled was the airship's first visit to Goodyear's British headquarters at Wolverhampton. In advance, the public relations department informed the press in all the areas over which the airship would fly of its probable time of appearance, and also gave them plenty of airship information.

Along the route, the airship flew over the Royal Agricultural Show at Kenilworth, which had been opened that day by the Queen. This resulted in early television coverage of the visit to Wolverhampton.

On arrival at Goodyear headquarters, three days were allocated for flying activities. The first was the company's directors, local dignitaries, the press, radio, and television. The second day was given over to top dealers invited by the sales department, and this proved to be a tremendous promotional event for the company. The third day was devoted to employee flights.

Interest in the *Europa* came not only from the media—including leading motoring magazines interested in its nonpollutant qualities—but from every walk of life, including schoolchildren, businessmen, academics, politicians, and industrialists, underlining the universal public interest created. Subsequently, wherever the *Europa* flew, it proved to be both the gainer of goodwill and an oustanding symbol of identification for the company.

AMERICAN RED CROSS

In 1979 the Austin chapter of the American Red Cross asked the University of Texas Public Relations Sequence to aid in conducting a survey as to the perception of metropolitan residents as to the role and function of the Red Cross. Students in a public relations class designed a questionnaire, identified a random sample, and conducted telephone interviews that indicated citizens in the Austin area were aware of the disaster-relief function of the Red Cross but were unaware of most of the other services provided. One of the Austin chapter's major programs, the water safety and swim program, was associated with another sponsor.

Two public relations student internships were arranged with the Red Cross for the development of feature articles about the various services. Attractive low-budget newsletters telling about Red Cross activities were also produced and distributed. Plans were also started for an observance of the hundredth anniversary of the American Red Cross in 1981.

The anniversary celebration was recognized as a vehicle for mass media coverage that could aid in identifying the role and function of the Red Cross in the public mind. Therefore, two functions were planned. One was an anniversary observance ceremony held in the city's largest shopping mall. Red Cross flags were hung from the top of the mall corridor, a major department store decorated a window with mannequins in WWI and WWII Red Cross and military uniforms, and Red Cross flags flew from the mall's outside flagpoles. A stage was set up with a billboard-size Red Cross centennial poster used as a backdrop. Exhibits were placed near the stage. A high school band and a military honor guard opened the short ceremony, which included state government representatives and a University of Texas quartet dressed in Red Cross uniforms from different time periods. Two of Austin's television stations covered the ceremony. The third network-affiliated station arrived late, but filmed the decorated mall and the live exhibits, which included blood pressure examinations.

The second function was held on the birthday of the establishment of the Austin chapter (now known as Centex) of the American Red Cross. It included a brief ceremony which included the presentation of the colors by a military honor guard and comments by the Austin mayor, a county official, and Red Cross officials and volunteers. Although the event's purpose was to express appreciation for volunteer service, it also attracted television coverage.

The two events acquired thousands of dollars in television coverage, which included information about the services provided by the Austin chapter of the American Red Cross.

The object to be learned from this example is the importance of research to publicity planning. Once the needs are known, courses of action can be developed that specifically address the problems.

PUBLIC RELATIONS AS A DEFENSIVE TOOL

Procter & Gamble, one of the United State's largest manufacturers with annual sales of more than $11 billion, ran into an unusual problem with the symbol that the company has used as a trademark since 1851. The circular symbol represents the man-in-the-moon with 13 stars representing the original 13 colonies in the United States. The man-in-the-moon was a popular symbol at the time the trademark was established.

Somehow a rumor started in the western United States that the firm's 131-year-old corporate symbol shows sympathy for the devil. Suddenly the firm began receiving hundreds of calls and letters from people who claimed they had either seen a corporate executive on a national television talk show relate that the symbol shows the company's ties to worship of Satan or had been told the information at their church.

In addition to responding to the inquiries with the facts, Procter & Gamble has begun an aggressive program that includes the sending of letters to every newspaper, television, and radio station in the localities where the rumor has spread. In addition regional and national church leaders of various denominations are being contacted and their help is asked in stopping the rumors. The Procter & Gamble mailings explain the origin of the crescent moon symbol and include a letter from the host of the national talk show explaining that no Procter & Gamble executive has ever appeared on his program to discuss satanism.

THE WOOLLY BEARS' PICNIC

One of the problems with handling public relations for a pest-control company is that of educating the public and encouraging them to take action. The public must be informed that products or services are available to deal with specific pests.

A plague of the "woolly bear" grubs of the carpet beetle *(Anthrenas verbasci)* was reported by a local newspaper in England. Alarmed householders called a meeting to discuss the problem. After fruitless contact with the local public health department, the local Rentokil pest-control surveyor and products salesman were asked to help, and this alerted Rentokil to the public relations potential of the situation.

A public meeting was organized at which an entomologist from the company's laboratories addressed two hundred people, followed by questions and a discussion lasting two hours. A local television crew then interviewed the entomologist, filmed a photogenic housewife/secretary using Rentokil spraying and dusting equipment, and even obtained film of the grubs themselves.

Later, network television conducted an interview, and the following day most national daily and major provincial newspapers gave the problem coverage. BBC Radio London and Radio Manchester recorded items on the subject, and *Practical Householder* and *Do-It-Yourself* both published short articles.

The effect was an increase in carpet beetle treatments all over England. Massive sales of Rentokil products resulted, and six times more mothproofer was sold than in the same period of the previous year—completely exhausting the factory's stock.

Apart from increased sales, decisive public relations activity at the right time gave an invaluable boost to Rentokil's image only a few months before the company went public.

THE CASE OF NETTINGSDORF

West of the Vienna–Salzburg Autobahn, near the Upper Austrian capital of Linz, there is one of the most modern paper factories in Europe. But only a few years ago no one had much faith in its future.

Three factors caused this pessimism: unfavorable public opinion caused by evil-smelling effluent waste, difficulties in recruiting young academic staff, and the pressing need for large-scale investment which could not be met from the company's own resources.

The pollution problem was such that, especially during low-pressure weather, the whole area was permeated by a very strong odor which completely antagonized the neighboring population. The local indignation was intensified by a whispering campaign based on the rumor that animal carcasses were being burnt, and there was a campaign in the local press encouraging public committees and politicians to clamor for the closure of the factory.

The recruitment of academic junior staff was a problem because the company was little known and had no image at the local universities. Consequently, it was not attractive for university graduates.

Large-scale investment was needed to enable the factory to be competitive, to assure its future, and to bring it up to European standards. A local bank syndicate was approached, but was rather hesitant to invest money in a company that was not very well known in economic circles and was hampered by the negative image caused by its pollution problems and recruitment difficulties.

At this stage a massive public relations campaign was started, its first efforts being directed toward improving public opinion in order to stop the demands for closing down the factory. Journalists, politicians, and local population had to be informed objectively about the origin of the evil-smelling waste, its extent, and the countermeasures that had already been introduced.

The success of this campaign was soon evident. Once people knew that the waste was not poisonous and that effective steps were being taken to reduce it to a minimum, the demands for closing down the factory were no longer heard. On the contrary, the public started to commend—and still commends—the fact that Nettingsdorf is a factory that fights pollution, at considerable cost.

A parallel campaign was initiated to improve contact with the universities. Discussions and factory tours showed students the company's up-to-date and far-seeing management, and a number of them were made familiar with the work and the problems in Nettingsdorf through a series of research contracts.

Within a relatively short period the image of Nettingsdorf at the universities became synonymous with an intellectual atmosphere and the possibilities of professional advancement; thus, the recruitment of young academic staff was assured.

During the whole period, an extensive press campaign informed economic circles and the public of Nettingsdorf's problems and its efforts to reach European standards. The media reported these promising developments, commending the management's forward planning and emphasizing the economic importance of the factory for the Upper Austrian area. All these factors contributed to the elimination of their last difficulty, a loan involving millions was granted, and the investment program could be realized.

Appropriate public relations measures not only saved the company from ruin, but enabled it to reach such standards that it is frequently cited as a model company.

COMMUNITY RELATIONS IN THE HIGHLANDS

Until 1971 Britain only had two aluminum smelter plants, both owned by British Aluminum (BA), and both situated in the Highlands of Scotland, where cheap electricity, used in large quantities for the electrolytic reduction of aluminum, was available from hydroelectric power stations.

With the advent of nuclear generation on a commercial scale, the

British government in 1967 invited four companies to submit proposals for the building of a new aluminum smelter.

By 1968 there were only two contenders, BA and Alcan, both of whom had purchased options on adjacent farms just outside the little town of Invergordon in Ross and Cromarty, Scotland. The town was ideally situated on firm building land next to a fine, undeveloped deep-water natural harbor; it had good road and rail links, and a plentiful supply of local labor caused by the closure of what was at one time a major naval dockyard.

Alcan mounted a powerful and expensive public relations campaign, including full-page advertisements in the Scottish daily papers and a massive mailing of a specially produced glossy brochure. BA, without the budget to undertake this type of campaign, concentrated on press relations and establishing contacts with significant people and organizations at local, regional, and national levels. In the end, BA's politically oriented campaign proved more successful than the methods adopted by Alcan, for in July 1968 the government awarded the contract to BA.

Immediately, an information campaign was drawn up designed to put over BA as an essentially Highlands company, and to create an atmosphere of cooperation and of consideration for local feelings.

The first shot in the campaign was the mailing of a facsimile-signed letter from BA's new managing director to 20,000 homes in the area, introducing the company and stating its broad plans. This was followed by a traveling exhibition under the guidance of a retired BA employee from the Fort William smelter. This kilted, Gaelic-speaking former town councillor did much to dispel a wide variety of misapprehensions, and he later became permanently reemployed as community relations officer. He also distributed thousands of leaflets about the company; these leaflets were subsequently used for general public information. All schools in the area were offered material on aluminum in general and smelters in particular, the company's bimonthly magazine had its internal distribution selectively enlarged to include significant local individuals.

A four-week campaign of advertising in the five local weeklies and the regional daily was launched, and an open town meeting was held in Invergordon, where five hundred people saw a film based on the older West Highlands smelter, and booklets were distributed. Immediately after the meeting a single-sheet card was published for distribution to local people and tourists through council offices, banks, hotels, clubs, and other places.

By the end of 1968 contractors had been appointed. Realizing that the relationships and attitudes created—or damaged—by the contractors during the two-and-a-half-year construction period would critically affect the company's long-term position in the community, BA's public relations officer drew up what was called an expression of policy, which was adopted by BA's top management and endorsed by the contractor's managing director. This was displayed on all staff notice boards and in every executive's office, and was given to every construction engineer appointed to the contract. This expression of policy was not openly publicized, but served quietly as a touchstone for community-relations decisions.

There then followed a series of promotions at local show jumping and agricultural events, including the presentations of an aluminum flagpole to the Invergordon Games and a new aluminum bardic crown for the Mod, the Scots version of a bard or minstrel.

Along with carefully selected financial contributions to the social life of the area, BA announced in October 1969 a grant to Aberdeen University for the study of the social and economic changes initiated by the smelter. Visits to the London headquarters of BA were arranged for local dignitaries, and VIPs from Edinburgh and Westminster visited the site.

A regular duplicated *Smelter Bulletin* was produced and distributed locally with details of progress on construction, and this bulletin later dealt with recruitment plans, training proposals, and other topics requiring public understanding.

Friendly contact was maintained with local members of Parliament, and good relations were maintained with the media so that a steady stream of news articles, background filming for television, and radio and TV interviews were ensured.

It was the company's policy to try to enter into a genuine dialogue with those who opposed its activities, and in most cases it was merely a question of reassuring groups that their fears were unnecessary and unfounded. Such it was with the Scottish Woodland Owners' Association, the Nature Conservancy and the Scottish Wild-Life Trust. However, the National Farmers' Union proved more formidable opponents. Their major worry was the possibility of damage to dairy cattle by fluorosis as a result of gaseous and particulate effluent settling on herbage. The company entered into an agreement for a procedure to handle claims for compensation, and monitoring points were established over a wide area.

BA even arranged for a Ministry of Agriculture veterinary expert to address NFU members on the causes and detection of fluorosis cattle, so that the farmers could judge the prospects on the basis of facts rather than hearsay.

BA's stated intention from the first was to recruit and train as many men from the immediate area of the region as possible for the predominantly semiskilled work in the smelter.

Numerically, there was no problem. BA established job specifications and selection procedures of a degree of sophistication totally unfamiliar in the Highlands, and its meticulous training program became widely known.

However, the first response to recruitment was lukewarm. There became apparent a slight social stigma against applying for jobs through the local Department of Employment, and there was even a fear that failure to get a place might be a social black mark.

A young research worker from Aberdeen University pinpointed the attitudes, and it was decided to set up a series of evening clinics in hotels around the area to which job applicants could go individually. After private and relaxed personal interviews, they were then either directed to the DE or invited to apply direct for a job, depending on the nature of the work.

The economic recession in the western world, which persisted throughout 1970 and 1971, hit aluminum companies everywhere. Rather than cutting prices and fighting for a share of a temporarily diminished market, these companies responded by cutting back on existing production and halting further expansion.

This meant that in May 1971, when the smelter was ready to go, there was already too much metal on the market.

This was a sad anticlimax, and it was decided to start operating at half capacity. It was felt that it would be inapprorite to spend money on a gala opening at a time when the company was cutting costs everywhere to ride out the economic storm. It had originally been hoped that there would be a royal opening, but in the circumstances the secretary of state for Scotland graced a minor ceremony; again, this was a compromise, as he could only visit the plant three weeks ahead of start-up.

The gratifying press, radio, and TV coverage in these pathetic circumstances was at least evidence of the value of nurturing relations with the media over the three years since the start of operations.

The BA approach to the problem of introducing a major industry into a remote agricultural area has worked to the benefit of the community, other industrial newcomers, and the company itself.

IMPROVING A COMPANY IMAGE
THROUGH GOOD COMMUNITY RELATIONS

Many of the larger multinational companies have found that a useful way of creating goodwill with their various publics—whether they be the local neighborhood or on a national or international level—and showing that the company is both aware and actively doing something about its social obligations in a community, is to sponsor art and education. This may be through touring or permanent exhibitions, trust foundations, or financial grants for student research scholarships.

Although the concept of a rich member of society sponsoring the poor student or artist for their mutual benfit is as old as art and education itself, it is only in the last decade or more that its public relations potential in a modern society has been fully realized.

The Peter Stuyvesant Foundation, the Courtauld Institute, and many large corporations have permanent art exhibitions. Several hotel chains, notably the Hilton group, have regular exhibitions of contemporary art.

This form of community relations need not be so lavish as those mentioned above. The Platignum Pen Company of Great Britain has for many years held a national handwriting contest for British schoolchildren, and examples of sponsorship on relatively small budgets are given below.

Objects: USA

The Johnson Wax Collection of Contemporary Arts, after a two-year tour of the United States and eighteen months in Europe, went to the City of Birmingham Museum and Art Gallery for four weeks in September of 1973. It was the only showing in England, and Johnson Wax decided to sponsor a Birmingham and District Schools' Crafts Competition. With the cooperation of the local education authorities, more than five hundred schools were invited to take part.

The competition was divided into three age groups, and entries were invited for objects made from any craft material in two- or three-dimensional form. The prizes included a weekend trip to Brussels, cash awards, and trophies.

The response and the standard of work submitted was so high that the museum's keeper of the department of art decided to put on an exhibition of the major works after the prizes had been awarded.

3M Research Fellowship

Environmental pollution has hit South Wales harder than many other industrialized areas. Mining and heavy industry have taken much from the rich soil without putting anything back.

3-M has manufactured in South Wales for more than twenty years, and in 1973 they felt it was time for them to make a really positive contribution to pollution control. They decided to sponsor a postgraduate scholar at the University College of Swansea to study for a Master of Science degree on the reclamation of derelict land in the lower Swansea Valley for amenity use.

In announcing their decision, 3M stated that "in the UK, 3M has its part to play as a responsible corporate member of society. Sponsorships such as this are an expression of the concern 3M feels for the communities in which it operates and the environment as a whole."

Art and Culture

The important Krupp Group of West Germany, which is well known for its heavy engineering and many other industrial enterprises, has for some time been sponsoring an interesting public relations exercise centered around the beautiful Villa Hugel in Essen, where the company stages a series of important art exhibitions and other cultural activities.

During the past ten years there has been a series of exceptional art exhibitions in the Villa Hugel. These have illustrated the art of many different countries, including Bulgaria, Iran, Egypt, India, Poland, Hungary, and the Soviet Union.

The cooperation between the board of Krupp and the government and leading personalities in the country of origin of these exhibitions has led to a happy relationship which has enabled Krupp to develop its trading interest in these countries. However, the art exhibitions have been of such high quality that they have been an end in themselves, and have served as a fine way of using the beautiful villa and the worldwide resources that only a company the size of Krupp can provide.

Promotion of Motorail

The public relations department of British Rail regularly organizes tailor-made campaigns to promote specific services. Motorail campaigns have been particularly successful.

The Motorail network, offering forty services and linking the main cities with the important holiday areas of England, Scotland, Ireland, and Wales, enables a motorist and his family or friends to travel on the same train as their car. This saves the long and tiresome journey along crowded roads to reach the holiday destination.

All overnight services include sleeping accommodations, and restaurant or snack-bar facilities are available on most day trains.

On the journey to Perth, the family can travel from London overnight and complete the 450 miles in about nine hours. This can save two days' motoring and overnight hotel accommodations. Prices are competitive. West Country journeys takes about five hours. Some Motorail services connect with ferries to Ireland and the Continent.

The Motorail campaign runs from October to February, with continuous support and maintenance of press contacts throughout the year. Basic material consists of a description of Motorail services, map of the network, a Motorail timetable, a list of main services, and photographs. An attractive press pack is sent out to all members of the Guild of Travel Writers, other known travel writers, and the motoring correspondents of leading newspapers and magazines.

The press pack is dispatched as soon as the Motorail timetable for the following season is available, usually in October or November. Prompt dispatch is the key, for by this time most leading newspapers and magazines are preparing their travel supplements for late December, January, and February.

Early in the spring, press notices are sent out about new services or facilities, and individual news items are fed to specific newspapers.

Regional railway public relations departments feed the press in their own territories within the total campaign.

The campaign is followed up continually by telephone calls, letters, and personal meetings with travel writers. Occasional exclusives are placed in the national daily and Sunday newspapers.

On one occasion the public relations department invited a manufacturing company to use the Motorail terminal at Olympia for their spring fashion photography. This resulted in massive provincial press coverage, featuring new fashions in a clearly recognizable Motorail setting.

Wide coverage is thus regularly secured. Market research shows that Motorail business secured through articles seen in newspapers and magazines account for nearly 10 percent of a business that now brings into BR nearly two million pounds a year.

Public Relations of Bricks and Mortar

An outstanding public relations success started as "Rockefeller's Folly." This was the name given in the early thirties to the ambitious scheme started by the late John D. Rockefeller, Jr. in the heart of New York City. This early example of urban renewal was started during the Depression, and roused great criticisms from architects and city planners alike. They complained that the architecture was undistinguished and the project had no civic purpose. Rockefeller kept quiet about the fact that he had originally leased the dozen acres on Fifth Avenue (between 48th and 51st Street) on behalf of a group planning a new home for the Metropolitan Opera, and that when the other backers had withdrawn after the 1929 crash he was left with this huge liability.

Unmoved by the criticism, Rockefeller pressed on with his plans for a modern city development that would be something new in city planning. He personally supervised construction work on the Center, and one day while he was standing on the pavement watching a huge steam shovel in an excavation a guard tapped him on the shoulder and told him to move on. Rockefeller moved on, but as a result of this experience he had windows cut in the high board walls around the site so that passersby could stop and watch the excavation work. The idea proved so popular that the Center's public relations department formed the Sidewalk Superintendents' Club, printed membership cards, and handed them out to the assembled watchers.

Financially speaking, the Rockefeller Center made a bad start, but now, more than forty years later, this has long been forgotten and the Center, further expanded, is both a financial success and a tourist mecca. Each day it is visited by more than 200,000 employees and visitors who enjoy its flower gardens, rest on its seats, watch skaters on its outdoor ice rink, and generally treat its handsome plaza as if it were a village square. Many New Yorkers believe that the plaza is city property, whereas it is a private street.

The success of the Rockefeller Center has encouraged ambitious urban renewal schemes in many other American cities. An example is the Prudential Center in Boston, a thirty-one-acre complex that includes a hotel and many other fine buildings replacing a dirty railroad yard. This and many other schemes owe much to Rockefeller's initial boldness in contributing a new concept to modern city development. This must surely rank high as a example of community public relations.

PUBLIC RELATIONS
IN LOCAL GOVERNMENT

Public relations in local government covers a very wide field. These three examples show how a public relations approach can assist local officials in anticipating public reaction to proposed measures, to answer unfair criticism, or to find a measure of agreement between local residents and the council on what is seemingly an intractable problem.

As an example of the first, one county official was considering reorganization of the fire service throughout its entire area, and the intended alterations included the complete closure of some fire stations and the resiting of others. The residents of an area feel safer if they are within reasonable distance of a fire station; but on the other hand, those in the immediate vicinity of a station do not take kindly to the disturbances naturally involved. Before the county council even submitted its proposals to its fire brigade committee or to the council as a whole, the chairman of the committee invited the entire press of the country to a conference attended by the chief fire officer, who explained the new proposals and answered questions. Thus the local press was able to explain the county's case and the need for local residents to take a more than parochial view of the problem. The press did this to very good effect. The chairman also announced his willingness to meet and discuss any objections on the spot in the particular area from whence they sprang. This was done in a few cases. The end result was that the reorganization was able to proceed smoothly and expeditiously, in direct contrast to the alternative method whereby authorities use statutory powers and proceed with projects regardless of public opinion and are, therefore, hampered at all stages by objections.

In another area in the same county, considerable criticism was being leveled at a local official in regard to one of its facilities for homeless families. This particular facility housed, in the main, what are considered large "problem" families, and the fault certainly did not lie with the local official. The county public relations officer invited the local television stations to the home, giving them a free hand to photograph anything they liked and to interview the occupants, with one request—that the chairman of the responsibile committee should be allowed to speak on the same broadcast. This was agreed, and after the bad conditions of the home and the quality of the occupants had been shown, the chairman made a clear statement regarding the local official's attitude. The criticism ended.

In another county a local official was seeking to establish a day school for mentally deficient children, and had finally chosen a large house in a middle-class residential area. In this particular area land was at a premium, suitable properties were almost nonexistent, and the house chosen was the only suitable one officials could find. As soon as the official's intention became known, a storm of protest rose from nearby residents. A meeting was called at which all the objectors could meet the chairman of the committee and with county officials. A county official gave deails of the unsuccessful search for other suitable sites or properties; the treasurer explained the financial aspect of the negotiations; the planning officer said his piece; and finally the medical officer described the type of school envisaged and the kind of unfortunate children who would attend it. The result was absolute stalemate, and might have remained so had not the objectors present been shocked into a realization of their responsibilities as citizens by the brutal question: "What would you like the council to do with these poor children, put them painlessly to sleep?"

OFF-BEAT PUBLIC RELATIONS

Gimmicks in public relations are justified only when there is a serious objective to be achieved. The supporting of a London double-decker bus on four Wedgwood china teacups was an excellent example of the successful public relations use of the gimmick, drawing attention to the remarkable strength of china despite the common belief that it is fragile.

There is certainly a place for gimmicks in public relations if used with great discretion; and, as in other aspects of public relations, care in planning and timing is the key to success.

19

Entering Public Relations

The preceding chapters have shown that public relations is not an exact science. To be a successful public relations practitioner demands a wide range of qualities and skills. The man or woman who aspires to reach the top rank needs to have sound judgment, personal integrity, a specialist knowledge of methods of communication, organizing ability of a high standard, and above all, a strong personality and capacity for leadership.

There is not room at the top for everybody, of course, and many people may prefer to specialize in a particular area of public relations such as films, exhibitions, or press relations. It is very helpful, however, to have had experience in more than one area of public relations before deciding to specialize. This is because no public relations function stands alone, and even in large departments where the work is sectionalized it is most useful to be able to double up in case of sickness or other emergency.

EDUCATIONAL REQUIREMENTS

In the past, men and women have entered the field of public relations with all types of academic backgrounds. Entry has been related more to an individual's communications skills than to his or her background. Recruitment, however, has concentrated on those with journalism degrees, since writing skill is of major importance and because organizations have first recognized their public relations needs in the areas of media relations and publication production.

Journalism schools have responded by adding public relations courses; today, some one hundred colleges and universities in the United States provide programs of study in public relations. The number of educational institutions with accredited programs also continues to increase.

Many of these programs are oriented toward media relations, whereas a communications management orientation is needed in which the student is thoroughly educated in the social sciences and management and familiarized with a broad range of communications knowledge.

Faculty members are needed in public relations with interdisciplinary backgrounds in anthropology, sociology, psychology, political science, management, and law as well as communications so that students will benefit from the diversity of approach to communications management. The diversity of academic backgrounds would also greatly benefit the profession by encouraging interdisciplinary approaches to public relations' research needs. The University of Free Berlin is one of the first universities to recognize the importance of such an approach. Other universities throughout the world can be expected to follow suit.

Students interested in public relations should keep in mind that a strong base is needed in the social sciences to understand how man communicates, adapts to change, behaves within small groups, organizations, and social structures. An understanding of man's needs, how he is motivated and persuaded, how he adapts to change, and how he functions best is also important.

In addition, the student needs to understand political systems and government and management theory.

Skill development is needed in writing, editing, speech, and graphic design in particular, with as much exposure as possible to the full range of communications techniques provided by today's technology.

The student also needs to acquaint himself or herself with the terminology of the business world through course work in business and with the terminology of the scientific community through the acquisition of course work in the basic sciences. The "working" language needed, however, will depend upon the field of public relations the student wishes to enter. Public relations students interested in the entertainment field, as an example, will find familiarity with the arts or sports more important than knowledge in other areas.

Therefore, educational requirements need flexibility, which indicates the specialization future degree programs in public relations will probably provide.

Academic training is by no means an assurance of a successful career in public relations, which demands qualities not easily measurable in examinations. The following list details some of these necessary qualities.

1. Abundant common sense.
2. First-class organizing ability.

3. Good judgment, objectivity, and keen critical ability.
4. Imagination and the ability to appreciate the other person's point of view.
5. Imperturbability.
6. An infinite capacity for detail.
7. A lively inquisitive mind.
8. Willingness to work long and inconvenient hours when necessary.
9. Resilience and a sense of humor.
10. Flexibility and the ability to deal with many different problems at the same time.

In addition to these qualities, it is essential to possess the ability to write well, and to be capable of correcting and copyreading other people's writing. The need for a positive personality has been mentioned and it is desirable that this should be supported by a pleasant voice and the ability for public speaking and persuasive presentation.

TRAINING COURSES

Hundreds of training courses are available to those wishing to improve their public relations skills. Most are offered by public relations' professional organizations. Universities and colleges are also offering adult education courses designed to teach entry-level skills in public relations or to expand one's knowledge in a specialized area such as fund raising or special event planning.

Internships and trainee programs are also available in many cases for those seeking to enter the public relations profession. The practical experience is highly desirable, particularly when combined with a sound academic program.

It is argued that practical experience as a journalist is a most desirable attribute in anyone wishing to enter public relations. This may be true of those who wish to make a career in press relations, but since so much of the work lies outside the press field there is no logical reason why a journalist should necessarily make a good public relations practitioner. Journalism does, however, develop certain habits of thought and actions such as objectivity, resourcefulness, and breadth of vision, which are valuable in public relations.

A thorough working knowledge of the press is essential to those engaged in public relations, but it is possible to acquire this without having actually worked on a newspaper.

A CAREER FOR WOMEN

Public relations is one of the careers that offer equal opportunities to women. Some of the women in public relations work for organizations or in fields that are characteristically feminine, such as the fashion or the food industries, but others work for public utilities and industry. In many instances they are heads of public relations departments, and there is no reason why women should remain in subordinate positions in public relations when they have the ability and desire to reach the top.

In a number of instances in the past, young women wishing to enter public relations have trained as shorthand-typist/secretaries and have joined public relations companies or departments to do secretarial work. This method of obtaining a foothold in public relations had some merit in the past when there were few opportunities of obtaining practical experience, but it is not to be recommended today except in cases where a young woman feels she would like to observe public relations from the inside before deciding to make it her career.

FIVE DEADLY SINS

A careful study of this book should have given a clear impression of the do's and don'ts of public relations, but a fitting conclusion to this chapter may be a list of five "deadly sins" to be avoided by all those who wish to make a successful career in public relations:

1. Never speak about public relations in highfalutin mumbo jumbo.
2. Do not seek personal publicity.
3. Never apologize for the views of the chairman or other chief executives.
4. Never patronize or talk down to the press.
5. Never think of or speak of press or media relations as being synonymous with public relations.

20

Public Relations Worldwide

Each year it becomes more evident that public relations activity cannot be confined by national frontiers. Nobody would deny that the United States has been preeminent in the public relations field both with regard to the number of practitioners and the quality of work. From 1946 onward, however, the ideas of public relations took firm root in the United Kingdom and have been adopted in many parts of Europe and the rest of the world outside the Soviet bloc.

The formation of the Institute of Public Relations in London in 1948 was an important landmark, and this was followed soon afterward by the beginning of informal discussions between public relations practitioners from a number of countries, including Norway, the Netherlands, France, the United States, and the United Kingdom. These informal meetings paved the way for the formation of the International Public Relations Association in 1955.

The first world public relations congress was held in Brussels in June 1958, and was attended by 250 practitioners from 23 countries. Since 1958 the Public Relations World Congresses have been held every three years: Venice, 1961; Montreal, 1964; Rio de Janeiro, 1967; Tel Aviv, 1970; Geneva, 1973; Boston, 1976; and London, 1979. The 9th Public Relations World Congress was held for the first time in Asia, in Bombay, in January 1982. The attendance was over 900 from 40 different countries. The International Public Relations Association holds its general assembly each year in different cities throughout the world.

The broad aims of IPRA are to do everything possible to raise world standards of public relations practice and to stimulate interest in education, training, and research. Membership is open to all fully qualified men and women in public relations whose work is of an international nature.

An interesting development has been the establishment of a number of regional public relations federations. For example, the European Confederation of Public Relations (CERP) was set up in May 1959 to examine standards of public relations training, education and practice in member countries, with a view to developing facilities and endeavoring to achieve the acceptance of common standards. Other regions have similarly seen the wisdom of forming regional federations. These include the Federation of African Public Relations Associations, the Federation of Asian Public Relations Organizations, the Inter-American Federation of Public Relations Associations, and the Pan Pacific Public Relations Federation. The following information illustrates the manner in which public relations practice is developing internationally.

AUSTRALIA

Companies, the government, and many other organizations now have public relations departments or use the services of consultants, or both. Public relations is recognized as an essential function of management—and a growing number of public relations executives are now operating at board level.

The Public Relations Institute of Australia had over nine hundred members in 1982 in varying membership categories of Fellow, Member, Associate, Affiliate, Student (Fellows and Students account for only about one hundred of these). Some public relations practitioners are still outside institute membership.

Public relations in Australia began as a separate function of management soon after the Second World War. In 1949 the state institute in New South Wales was formed; in the 1950s state institutes in Victoria, South Australia, and Queensland came into being; and there are now also state institutes in Tasmania, Western Australia, and in the Australian Capital Territory.

The national body entered the scene in 1960. National conventions are held every two years.

There are now two graduate courses in communications and public relations offered in New South Wales and one in Queensland; and certificate courses are available in Victoria and South Australia.

BELGIUM

The Centre Belge des Relations Publiques/Belgisch Centrum voor Public Relations (CBRP/BCPR) was formed in Brussels by a few enthusiasts in 1952, and public relations has made great strides in Belgium since that time. The Belgian association was responsible for the very successful world congress held in Brussels in 1958, and the introduction of the European Economic Community has also given an impetus to the use of public relations. The Belgian association is also growing at a steady rate.

Courses in public relations are held at the universities of Louvain, Brussels, and Ghent, as well as in business schools in Tournai, Ghent, and Antwerp.

The CBRP/BCPR organizes regular meetings in Brussels and other Belgian cities, and a course of practical public relations in Brussels.

CANADA

The Canadian Public Relations Society was formed in Montreal in 1948 as a society of Montreal practitioners. In the same year the Public Relations Association of Ontario was formed to meet the interests and needs of practitioners in the Toronto area. These two independent associations merged in 1953 to form the national body now known as the Canadian Public Relations Society, a fully bilingual body (English and French) incorporated under federal charter in 1957. The society now has about 1,500 members in 12 regional societies repersenting 9 provinces. There are a number of individual members located outside Canada.

The business of the society is conducted through its elected officers drawn from member societies all over Canada. The national office is located in Ottawa.

Since 1969 the society has conducted a voluntary accreditation program for its members. This involves following a recommended course of study, submitting a work sample, and undergoing both a written and oral examination. Applicants must have a minimum of five years' public relations experience, and be employed full time in public relations. A successful candidate becomes an accredited member and is entitled to the suffix APR.

A number of community colleges have developed courses in public relations work. CPRS is working with educational institutions in providing guidelines and uniformity to the teaching of public relations. It helped to establish a four-year Bachelor of Public Relations course at Mount Saint Vincent University, Halifax, NS, in 1977.

DENMARK

Public relations in Denmark is still in a developmental state. Because of the lack of a local equivalent, the English term has been incorporated in the Danish language; this, however, has led to some confusion, and today *public relations* is used in a large number of contexts. The public in general does not know what the term stands for, and in industrial and business circles it is most often thought of as a form of advertising, or as merely press-agentry. This is a problem common to many countries, however.

The large Danish companies are more advanced, and public relations departments are found in most of them—normally called information departments. It is significant, however, that the practitioners in the large companies very seldom call themselves public relations personnel, but use a variety of other titles.

The problem of public relations in Denmark stems from the fact that there is no basic education for practitioners. The Danish Public Relations Society was established in 1961 and has over a hundred members—51 percent employed in industry and commerce, 9 percent in trade organizations, 11 percent in finance and insurance, 9 percent in government and municipial organizations, and 6 percent in other sectors; 14 percent of the members are listed as consultants, but some of them are part-time.

In 1963 DPRK adopted a denfiition of public relations that is in line with the IPRA definition, and in 1964 a code of conduct was accepted by all members. Membership is limited to applicants who are full-time practitioners. No examinations are required for membership, but the DPRK runs courses, and most new members attend these.

FRANCE

Over a hundred years ago, the French philosopher and sociologist Auguste Comte wrote: "A business enterprise should be open and clear like a glass house for all to see. There is a duty on those managing businesses to enlighten public opinion on their activities." These words were remembered by the group of ten pioneers who formed the first public relations society in France, and they called it La Maison de Verre—the Glass House. This was in 1949, a time when large industrial companies in France were beginning to take an interest in public relations.

Two years later a professional association was formed—L'Association Professionnelle des Conseillers et Cadres en Relations Publiques et Sociales. A few years later this name was changed to L'Association Française des Relations Publiques (AFREP) to give a clearer indication of its composition. AFREP groups bring together those actually engaged in professional public relations practice.

Another professional association is the Syndicat National des Conseils en Relations Publiques.

Teaching of public relations is well developed in France. The University of Paris (Sorbonne) has a branch, the CELSA, which trains practitioners in a two-year course. The students must have at least a *licence* (equivalent to a master's degree) in order to be accepted. There are also several Institutes Universitaires de Technologie (IUT) which produce specialists at a lower level than the CELSA (two years' training just after the Baccalauréat.) Two private schools, the Institut des Relations Publiques and the Ecole Française des Attachés de Presse, also provide training for public relations students, while a number of other organizations have courses in public relations. In 1973 the Sorbonne started to organize seminars in public relations for middle and top management.

In 1970 five associations dealing with public relations in France— AFREP, SNCRP, UNAP (Union Nationale des Attachés de Presse), SYNAP (Syndicat National des Attachés de Presse), and UJEF (Union des Journaux d'Entreprise de France) decided to create the Federation Française des Relations Publiques.

GERMANY

Public relations activities in West Germany developed later than in other European countries, but we are now making rapid progress. One of the difficulties was that *public relations* cannot be translated into German, and hence many organizations practiced public relations without using the term. Other terms were used, such as *Meinungspflege, Kontaktpflege, Vertrauenswerbung,* and *Offentlichkeitsarbeit.* Despite these varying terms, the work includes the basic public relations function such as press relations, consumer relations, community relations, and stockholder relations.

A help for their definition of public relations is the *Kleines ABC der Public Relations,* which was published in 1972.

After the Second World War many industrial and other companies began to realize the importance of organized public relations, but it was not until 1958 that the Deutsche Public Relations Gesellschaft (DPRG) was formed.

Most companies have their own public relations departments, but there are independent consultants and special agencies and also branches of a few American public relations companies. Some advertising agencies also have public relations departments.

Every two years the DPRG awards the *Goldene Brucke* (golden bridge) for the best public relations activity in three categories—industry, independent consultants and special agencies, and governmental and municipal authorities. Also, every two years it honors the outstanding public relations activity for the country with the *Johann Gottfried von Herder Preis,* but this award is not given to officials.

In 1980 the Freie Universität Berlin initiated the development of a public relations curriculum at the master's degree level. The academic program is being taught by an interdisciplinary faculty with backgrounds in the social sciences, journalism, and law.

NETHERLANDS

Informal meetings of a number of leading press officers immediately after WWII led to a more formal association, Genootschap voor Openbaar Contact, on March 1, 1946. This society is considered to be the official predecessor of the Nederlands Genootschap voor Public Relations (Netherlands Society of Public Relations), which received royal assent in 1952. In 1979 the name was changed to NGPR, Vereniging voor Public Relations en Voorlichting (Association for Public Relations and Information).

Membership of the NGPR is open to public relations and information officers of good reputation with Dutch nationality. Full members are those in responsible positions who work fulltime in public relations or information. They must adhere to the NGPR Code of Ethics, breaches of which can lead to action by a disciplinary committee. Of the more than five hundred members in 1980, about forty consultants form the separate Association of Public Relations Consultancies (VPRA), which is linked with the NGPR.

Various private institutions organize regular orientation conferences on public relations for managers or companies and organizations. Two institutions have a forty-hour course for public relations practitioners who want more background and practical help. A professional training course (140 hours) is organized by three institutions every year. The final examination, which has been recognized by the government since 1967, is held under the auspices of the NGPR.

In 1978 the NGPR was allowed to appoint a professor in the theory of public relations at the State University of Utrecht. Since then, public relations has become an optional study on the academic level in the Netherlands. Postacademic courses are also now being provided in Utrecht.

In the last fifteen years there has been a growing interest in public relations and information in the Netherlands. The NGPR holds a annual conference and regular meetings. A magazine called *PR en Voorlichting* is published monthly. In addition, a more scientific magazine, *Cahiers Public Relations en Voorlichting,* is published quarterly in cooperation with the Flemish section of the BCPR.

The NGPR is a active member of CERP.

SPAIN

Public relations departments, set up within industrial companies and companies offering services, started to come into being in Spain in 1958. In 1960 the first Spanish company entirely devoted to public relations was set up. Since then the use of public relations has widened, and by 1974 there were more than three thousand professionals working in public relations.

Although until a few years ago most companies did not feel a need for public relations, more and more organizations are now realizing that it is a necessary element for success. Whereas previously management saw public relations as a sales tool geared to immediate results rather than as a service involving all a company's activities, rapid industrial development in Spain has caused a series of problems which can only be solved by the application of public relations techniques. More and more companies are calling on the services of outside consultants and eventually forming their own public relations departments.

IRELAND

Two decades ago it was only government or semigovernmental organizations in Ireland that took public relations seriously, and it was on the guidance of their public relations officers or information officers that the Public Relations Institute of Ireland (PRI) depended. More recently, however, public relations thinking has become more commercially oriented and membership of the PRI has dramatically increased. The PRI has become more international in outlook, and is a member of both IPRA and CERP; and it has also become more education conscious, with training courses for student members.

The significant growth in public relations activities in Ireland coincides with the country's economic expansion program and with Ireland's entry into the EEC. The future growth of public relations throughout the country seems assured.

ITALY

A new federation, the Federazione Relazioni Pubbliche Italiana (FERPI), was founded in 1970 from the merger of the former FIRP and FIERP organizations. FERPI groups have about six hundred members, all professionals, private counsellors, or managers of public relations offices of private and public concerns.

FERPI operates mainly for the advancement of the profession and recently started training courses for all its members.

In 1972 the Milan University of Modern Languages, with the approval of the Ministry of Public Education, set up a four-year course in public relations that leads to an officially recognized degree in public relations.

At present there are about fifty private agencies in Italy, about ten freelance consultants, and about 300 public relations managers—mostly in both privately and publicly owned industries and in public administration.

The image of public relations in Italy has improved during the last twenty years, but the profession has not yet been universally accepted or understood though it has been growing rapidly during the last few years.

UNITED STATES OF AMERICA*

The profession of public relations has made great strides in the United States in recent years. This has been due in part to the growing professionalism of its practitioners and to the influx into the field of young men and women trained in the universities for the practice of public relations. But major social trends have also helped to shape the course of public relations, with an intensification of its use and a recognition of its growing importance as an ancillary service to institutions and organizations of all kinds.

The broad structure of American society has emphasized the need for a sense of social responsibility by all enterprises, profit-making and nonprofit-making alike. All of them are more aware of public opinion in the planning of their courses of action. For example, public concern about environmental pollution has heightened public relations activities in all the fields that impinge on this. The consumer movement, too, has increased the use of public relations in all activities that affect the consumer.

Social responsibility is expected from all institutions that deal with the public, and the institutions respond either from a spirit of enlightened self-interest or else from some other motivation.

The public relations man or woman has under these circumstances become a more potent force in industry and commerce, interpreting public opinion to management and, in turn, helping to interpret corporate policies to the public.

Based on this situation, and with over half a century of practical

* This section has been contributed by Edward L. Bernays.

experience to draw upon, I have tried to develop what might be termed the ten essentials of public relations:

1. The practice of pubic relations is a profession—an art applied to a science. The public interest, not pecuniary motivation, is the primary consideration in its practice. The profession has its literature, its voluntary associations, and its educational curricula—all criteria of a profession.

2. Public relations concerns itself with the relations of a unit, an organization, or an individual with the publics on which it depends for its viability. Public relations advance covers adjustments to the public, information to the public, and persuasion to the public to accept a service or product.

3. The need for the public relations practitioner as a societal technician has been brought about by the revolution in transportation and communication, more widespread literacy, the increasingly complex network of communications, and the resultant greater participation by the public in the shaping of all institutions.

4. Effective public relations establishes a meeting point, to the highest degree of adjustment, between an organization and the publics upon which it depends.

5 Effective public relations is based on reality—not on images, whether true or false. Deeds and action that serve the public interest are the basis of sound public relations.

6. An organizations seeks public approval and support on the basis of the public interest. The public interest is the criterion by which a public relations professional accepts a client. He rejects the client who does not serve the public interest.

7. The public relations man first evaluates, by scientific public opinion research, the concords and discords between his client and his publics. He advises his client on the modification of attitude and actions that are indicated. He advises on information neeeded by the public to provide a basis for understanding and support. He advises on methods of persuasion necessary to gain public support.

8. Professional public relations practice depends on the application of social sciences (psychology, sociology, social psychology, public opinion, communications study, and semantics) to the problem at hand.

9. The public relations professional plays an important role in preparing the various segments of the society for coming developments—in order to prevent future shock.

10. The professional public relations man or woman is remunerated on the principle of *quantum meruit,* which sets the pattern in other professions.

21

How it All Began: Some Historical Notes

Public relations has been practiced sporadically since the earliest times, even though the name is of comparatively recent origin. Before discussing the modern history, it is interesting to recall some early examples of public relations activities in different parts of the world.

FROM GREEK AND ROMAN TIMES TO 1914

There is ample evidence in the records of the early Greek and Roman empires to show that great care and attention was devoted to the influencing of public opinion. Public relations in those far-off days appears to have been an integral part of government. The Romans dramatized the importance of public opinion in the slogan *vox populi, vox dei*—the vocie of the people is the voice of God.

In more recent history, the American Revolution was started by a small group of men, including Samuel Adams, Thomas Paine, Benjamin Franklin, Alexander Hamilton, and Thomas Jefferson, who used voice and pen to make a profound effect on the public opinion of their day. They circulated pamphlets, wrote in the press, lectured, and spread their ideas of revolt by word of mouth.

In England, the pamphleteers of the eighteenth century, men such as Jonathan Swift and Daniel Defoe, were using methods to propagate their ideas that had much in common with present-day public relations practice. This applies also to the work of Huxley to promote the evolutionary ideas of Darwin, and the writings of Charles Dickens to expose the social evils of his time.

There is no need to multiply examples to prove the point that public relations practice is nearly as old as the world itself. All that is new is the proliferation of the idea consequent on the industrialization and intensification of modern life and the availablity of the new means of communication. The former has created the need for public relations; the new mass media have provided the tools.

DEVELOPMENT IN THE UNITED STATES

The first actual use of the phrase *public relations* is thought to have been in 1807 when President Thomas Jefferson, drafting his Seventh Address to Congress in his own hand, scratched out the words *state of thought* in one place and wrote in *public relations* instead. It is to the United States of America, too, that the world owes the modern development of public relations, although Great Britain and other countries have proved apt pupils.

That colorful personality, Ivy L. Lee, left a poorly paid job as a reporter in 1903 and started as a press agent. His work as personal adviser to John D. Rockefeller, Jr., began in December 1914, but it was not until 1919 that he began to use the term *public relations*. Lee contributed many of the techniques and principles that characterize public relations today, and he was among the first to realize the fallacy of publicity unsupported by good works. His success in changing the public image of John D. Rockefeller, Sr., from a "greedy old capitalist" to a kindly old man who gave dimes to children and millions of dollars to charity, has become a legend.

The First World War gave public relations a big impetus in the USA. President Wilson set up the Committee on Public Information in response to a suggestion by a journalist friend, George Creel. The Creel committee grew into a vast enterprise which demonstrated the power of organized publicity.

Among many talented men and women working for the Creel committee was Edward L. Bernays, a nephew of Sigmund Freud. Bernays coined the term *public relations counsel,* and his book *Crystallising Public Opinion,* published in 1923, was the first full-length book dealing with public relations.

Between the wars there was a remarkable expansion of public relations activities in every walk of American life. The advent of the Second World War accelerated this tendency, and once again the government led the way with the formation of the Office of War Information under Elmer Davis. The OWI encouraged extensive expansion of public relations in the armed forces, in industry, and in allied fields. Many of today's leading practitioners served their apprenticeships in the gigantic public relations program that dwarfed the efforts of the earlier Creel committee.

United States presidents have had a major role in improving public understanding of the importance of public relations activity. President Andrew Jackson was the first to rely heavily on journalists for advice and staff assistance. President Franklin Delano Roosevelt used the radio for his famous fireside chats in order to build confidence and achieve support for his programs. The approach was used later by President John F. Kennedy with the new communication medium, television.

Public relations, although still misunderstood as a function by many in the United States, has grown rapidly as a professional area. The Public Relations Society of America, The International Association of Business Communicators, state public relations associations, and specialized public relations associations have increased their memberships one hundred percent or more during the past decade.

The growth of academic programs in public relations in colleges and universities throughout the United States and a growing student interest in public relations and the job opportunities that continue to develop for graduates has brought public relations in the U.S. to the point of professional recognition.

DEVELOPMENT IN GREAT BRITAIN

In Britain the first stirrings of organized public relations were probably the efforts made by the Insurance Commission in 1911, under the instructions of Lloyd George, to explain the National Insurance Act. The outbreak of war in 1914 led to a rapid expansion of official publicity in Britain and overseas, which was at first carried out by a number of separate bodies. By early in 1918 such publicity was conducted in the main by three organizations: the Ministry of Information, responsible for publicity work in Dominions and in Allied and neutral countries; the National War Aims Committee, which carried out patriotic propaganda in Britain; and a committee under Lord Northcliffe that was responsible for propaganda in enemy countries. This work was a mixture of public relations and propaganda.

These organizations were abolished after the war, but some of their functions were transformed to other departments, principally to the news department of the Foreign Office. In 1926 the establishment of the Empire Marketing Board marked the first use of public relations as we understand it today. The late Sir Stephen Tallents, founder president of the Institute of Public Relations, was selected to run the new venture, which had as its object "bringing the Empire alive to the mind of people in Britain." The EMB used films, posters, exhibitions, the press, and the BBC to publicize its objectives.

The work of the Empire Marketing Board was cut short by the onset of the serious economic crisis in the autumn of 1931. At short notice, the EMB was ordered to switch all its resources to the launching of a full-scale campaign in support of the prime minister's appeal to "Buy British." All media of communication were employed, and the campaign received widespread support. Its success surpassed expectations and proved—for the first time in Britain—the benefits that can come from a well-conceived and energetically administered public relations campaign.

Sir Stephen Tallents continued his policy of using the best available artists, filmmakers, and other experts when he became public relations officer to the post office in 1933. This appointment is thought by many to have been the first use of the term in the United Kingdom, having been taken by the postmaster-general the late Sir Kingsley Wood, from American practice.

At the outbreak of war in 1939 a Ministry of Information was again set up. This large-scale government public relations project was paralleled by the setting up of public relations units in all branches of the armed forced. The MOI made a massive contribution to the successful prosecution of the war, and the team of all talents produced some remarkably effective results. When the war ended it was decided to replace the MOI by a non-ministerial department, the Central Office of Information.

The appointment of a public relations officer by the National Association of Local Government Officers (now known as the National and Local Government Officers' Association) in 1937 was supplemented by a system of honorary district and branch public relations officers.

British industry did not show very much interest in public relations until 1945, but since then the increase in industrial public relations in the United Kingdom has been rapid.

APPENDIXES

Appendix A:

Codes of Professional Conduct and Ethics

PRSA CODE OF PROFESSIONAL STANDARDS

This Code, adopted by the PRSA Assembly, replaces a similar Code of Professional Standards for the Practice of Public Relations previously in force since 1954 and strengthened by revisions in 1959, 1963, and 1977.

Declaration of Principles

Members of the Public Relations Society of America base their professional principles on the fundamental value and dignity of the individual, holding that the free exercise of human rights, especially freedom of speech, freedom of assembly and freedom of the press, is essential to the practice of public relations.

In serving the intereste of clients and employers, we dedicate ourselves to the goals of better communication, understanding, and cooperation among the diverse individuals, groups and institutions of society.

We pledge:

To conduct ourselves professionally, with truth, accuracy, fairness, and responsibility to the public;

To improve our individual competence and advance the knowledge and proficiency of the profession through continuing research and education;

And to adhere to the articles of the Code of Professional Standards for the Practice of Public Relations as adopted by the governing Assembly of the Society.

Articles of the Code

These articles have been adopted by the Public Relations Society of America to promote and maintain high standards of public service and ethical conduct among its members.

1. A member shall deal fairly with clients or employers, past and present, with fellow practitioners and the general public.

2. A member shall conduct his or her professional life in accord with the public interest.

3. A member shall adhere to truth and accuracy and to generally accepted standards of good taste.

4. A member shall not represent conflicting or competing interests without the express consent of those involved, given after a full disclosure of the facts; nor place himself or herself in a position where the member's interest is or may be in conflict with a duty to a client, or others, without a full disclosure of such interests to all involved.

5. A member shall safeguard the confidences of both present and former clients or employers and shall not accept retainers or employment which may involve the disclosure or use of these confidences to the disadvantage or prejudice of such clients or employers.

6. A member shall not engage in any practice which tends to corrupt the integrity of channels of communication or the processes of government.

7. A member shall not intentionally communicate false or misleading information and is obligated to use care to avoid communication of false or misleading information.

8. A member shall be prepared to identify publicly the name of the client or employer on whose behalf any public communication is made.

9. A member shall not make use of any individual or organization purporting to serve or represent an announced cause, or purporting to be independent or unbiased, but actually serving an undisclosed special or private interest of a member, client, or employer.

10. A member shall not intentionally injure the professional reputation or practice of another practitioner. However, if a member has evidence that another member has been guilty of unethical, illegal, or unfair practices, including those in violation of this Code, the member shall present the information promptly to the proper authorities of the Society for action in accordance with the procedure set forth in Article XIII of the Bylaws.

11. A member called as a witness in a proceeding for the enforcement of this Code shall be bound to appear, unless excused for sufficient reason by the Judicial Panel.

12. A member, in performing services for a client or employer, shall not accept fees, commissions, or any other valuable consideration from anyone other than the client or employer in connection with those services without the express consent of the client or employer, given after a full disclosure of the facts.

13. A member shall not guarantee the achievement of specified results beyond the member's direct control.

14. A member shall, as soon as possible, sever relations with any organization or individual if such relationship requires conduct contrary to the articles of this Code.

Official Interpretations of the Code

Interpretation of Code Paragraph 2 which reads, "A member shall conduct his or her professional life in accord with the public interest."

> The public interest is here defined primarily as comprising respect for and enforcement of the rights guaranteed by the Constitution of the United States of America.

Interpretation of Code Paragraph 5 which reads, "A member shall safeguard the confidences of both present and former clients or employers and shall not accept retainers or employment which may involve the disclosure or use of these confidences to the disadvantage or prejudice of such clients or employers."

> This article does not prohibit a member who has knowledge of client or employer activities which are illegal from making such disclosures to the proper authorities as he or she believes are legally required.

Interpretation of Code Paragraph 6 which reads, "A member shall not engage in any practice which tends to corrupt the integrity of channels of communication or the processes of government."

1. Practices prohibited by this paragraph are those which tend to place representatives of media or government under an obligation to the the member, or the member's employer or client, which is in conflict with their obligations to media or government, such as:

   a. the giving of gifts of more than nominal value;

    b. any form of payment or compensation to a member of the media in order to obtain preferential or guaranteed news or editorial coverage in the medium;

    c. any retainer or fee to a media employee or use of such employee if retained by a client or employer, where the circumstances are not fully disclosed to and accepted by the media employer;

    d. providing trips for media representatives which are unrelated to legitimate news interest;

    e. the use by a member of an investment or loan or advertising commitment made by the member, or the members's client or employer, to obtain preferential or guaranteed coverage in the medium.

2. This Code paragraph does not prohibit hosting media or government representatives at meals, cocktails, or news functions or special events which are occasions for the exchange of news information or views, or the furtherance of understanding which is part of the public relations function. Nor does it prohibit the bona fide press event or tour when media or government representatives are given an opportunity for on-the-spot viewing of a newsworthy product, process, or event in which the media or government representatives have a legitimate interest. What is customary or reasonable hospitality has to be a matter of particular judgment in specific situations. In all of these cases, however, it is nor should be understood that no preferential treatment or guarantees are expected or implied and that complete independence always is left to the media or government representative.

3. This paragraph does not prohibit the reasonable giving or lending of sample products or services to media representatives who have a legitimate interest in the products or services.

Interpretation of Code Paragraph 13 which reads, "A member shall not guarantee the achievement of specified results beyond the member's direct control."

This Code paragraph, in effect, prohibits misleading a client or employer as to what professional public relations can accomplish. It does not prohibit guarantees of quality or service. But it does prohibit guaranteeing specific results which, by their very nature, cannot be guaranteed because they are not subject to the member's control. As an example, a guarantee that a news release will appear specifically in a particular publication would be prohibited. This paragraph should not be interpreted as prohibiting contingent fees.

An Official Interpretation of the Code
As It Applies to Political Public Relations

Preamble. In the practice of political public relations, a PRSA member must have professional capabilities to offer an employer or client quite apart from any political relationships of value, and members may serve their employer or client without necessarily having attributed to them the character, reputation, or beliefs of those they serve. It is understood that members may choose to serve only those interests with whose political philosophy they are personally comfortable.

Definition. "Political Public Relations" is defined as those areas of public relations which relate to:
   a. the counseling of political organizations, committees, candidates, or potential candidates for public office; and groups constituted for the purpose of influencing the vote on any ballot issue;
   b. the counseling of holders of public office;
   c. the management, or direction, of a political campaign for or against a candidate for political office; or for or against a ballot issue to be determined by voter approval or rejection;
   d. the practice of public relations on behalf of a client or an employer in connection with that client's or employer's relationships with any candidates or holders of public office with the purpose of influencing legislation or government regulation or treatment of a client or employer, regardless of whether the PRSA member is a recognized lobbyist;
   e. the counseling of government bodies, or segments thereof, either domestic or foreign.

Percepts.
   1. It is the responsibility of PRSA members practicing political public relations, as defined above, to be conversant with the various statutes, local, state, and federal, governing such activities and to adhere to them strictly. This includes, but is not limited to, the various local, state, and federal laws, court decisions and official interpretations governing lobbying, political contributions, disclosure, elections, libel, slander, and the like. In carrying out this repsonsibility, members shall seek appropriate counseling whenever necessary.

   2. It is also the responsibility of members to abide by PRSA's Code of Professional Standards.

   3. Members shall represent clients or employers in good faith, and while partisan advocacy on behalf of a candidate or public issue

187

may be expected, members shall act in accord with the public interest and adhere to truth and accuracy and to generally accepted standards of good taste.

4. Members shall not issue descriptive material or any advertising or publicity information or participate in the preparation or use thereof which is not signed by responsible persons or is false, misleading or unlabeled as to its source, and are obligated to use care to avoid dissemination of any such material.

5. Members have an obligation to clients to disclose what remuneration beyond their fees they expect to receive as a result of their relationship, such as commissions for media advertising, printing, and the like, and should not accept such extra payment without their client's consent.

6. Members shall not improperly use their positions to encourage additional future employment or compensation. It is understood that successful campaign directors or managers, because of the performance of their duties and the working relationship that develops, may well continue to assist and counsel, for pay, the successful candidate.

7. Members shall voluntarily disclose to employers or clients the identity of other employers or clients with whom they are currently associated and whose interests might be affected favorably or unfavorably by their political repersentation.

8. Members shall respect the confidentiality of information pertaining to employers or clients even after the relationships cease, avoiding future associations wherein insider information is sought that would give a desired advantage over a member's previous clients.

9. In avoiding practices which might tend to corrupt the processes of government, members shall not make undisclosed gifts of cash or other valuable considerations which are designed to influence specific decisions of voters, legislators, or public officials on public matters. A business lunch or dinner, or other comparable expenditure made in the course of communicating a point of view or public position, would not constitute such a violation. Nor, for example, would a plant visit designed and financed to provide useful background information to an interested legislator or candidate.

10. Nothing herein should be construed as prohibiting members from making legal, properly disclosed contributions to the candidates, party, or referenda issues of their choice.

11. Members shall not, through the use of information known to be false or misleading, conveyed directly or through a third party, intentionally injure the public reputation of an opposing interest.

An Official Interpretation of the Code
As It Applies to Financial Public Relations

This interpretation of the Society Code as it applies to financial public relations was originally adopted in 1963 and amended in 1972 and 1977 by action of the PRSA Board of Directors. "Financial public relations" is defined as "that area of public relations which relates to the dissemination of information that affects the understanding of stockholders and investors generally concerning the financial position and prospects of a company, and includes among its objectives the improvements of relations between corporations and their stockholders." The interpretation was prepared in 1963 by the Society's Financial Relations Committee working with the Securities and Exchange Commission and with the advice of the Society's Legal Counsel. It is rooted directly in the Code with the full force of the Code behind it and a violation of any of the following paragraphs is subject to the same procedures and penalties as violation of the Code.

1. It is the responsibility of PRSA members who practice financial public relations to be thoroughly familiar with and understand the rules and regulations of the SEC and the laws which it administers, as well as other laws, rules, and regulations affecting financial public relations, and to act in accordance with their letter and spirit. In carrying out this responsibility, members shall also seek legal counsel, when appropriate, on matters concerning financial public relations.

2. Members shall adhere to the general policy of making full and timely disclosure of corporate information on behalf of clients or employers. The information disclosed shall be accurate, clear, and understandable. The purpose of such disclosure is to provide the investing public with all material information affecting security values or influencing investment decisions. In complying with the duty of full and timely disclosure, members shall present all material facts, including those adverse to the company. They shall exercise care to ascertain the facts and to disseminate only informa- which they believe to be accurate. They shall not knowingly omit information, the omission of which might make a release false or misleading. Under no circumstances shall members participate in

any activity designed to mislead, or manipulate the price of a company's securities.

3. Members shall publicly disclose or release information promptly so as to avoid the possibility of any use of the information by any insider or third party. To that end, members shall make every effort to comply with the spirit and intent of the timely disclosure policies of the stock exchanges, NASD, and the Securities and Exchange Commission. Material information shall be made available to all on an equal basis.

4. Members shall not disclose confidential information the disclosure of which might be adverse to a valid corporate purpose or interest and whose disclosure is not required by the timely disclosure provisions of the law. During any such period of nondisclosure members shall not directly or indirectly (a) communicate the confidential information to any other person or (b) buy or sell or in any other way deal in the company's securities where the confidential information may materially affect the market for the security when disclosed. Material information shall be disclosed publicly as soon as its confidential status has terminated or the requirement of timely disclosure takes effect.

5. During the registration period, members shall not engage in practices designed to precondition the market for such securities. During registration the issuance of forecasts, projections, predictions about sales and earnings, or opinions concerning security values or other aspects of the future performance of the company, shall be in accordance with current SEC regulations and statements of policy. In the case of companies whose securities are publicly held, the normal flow of factual information to shareholders and the investing public shall continue during the registration period.

6. Where members have any reason to doubt that projections have an adequate basis in fact, they shall satisfy themselves as to the adequacy of the projections prior to disseminating them.

7. Acting in concert with clients or employers, members shall act promptly to correct false or misleading information or rumors concerning clients' or employers' securities or business whenever they have reason to believe such information or rumors are materially affecting investor attitudes.

8. Members shall not issue descriptive materials designed or written in such a fashion as to appear to be, contrary to fact, an inde-

pendent third party endorsement or recommendation of a company or a security. Whenever members issue material for clients or employers, either in their own names or in the name of someone other than clients or employers, they shall disclose in large type and in a prominent position on the face of the material the source of such material and the existence of the issuer's client or employer relationship.

9. Members shall not use inside information for personal gain. However, this is not intended to prohibit members from making bona fide investments in their company's or client's securities insofar as they can make such investments without the benefit of material inside information.

10. Members shall not accept compensation which would place them in a position of conflict with their duty to a client, employer, or the investing public. Members shall not accept stock options from clients or employers, nor accept securities as compensation at a price below market price except as part of an overall plan for corporate employees.

11. Members shall act so as to maintain the integrity of channels of public communication. They shall not pay or permit to be paid to any publication or other communications medium any consideration in exchange for publicizing a company, except through clearly recognizable paid advertising.

12. Members shall in general be guided by the PRSA Declaration of Principles and the PRSA Code of Professional Standards for the Practice of Public Relations of which this Code is an official interpretation.

IPRA CODE OF PROFESSIONAL CONDUCT

The following code of conduct was adopted by the International Public Relations Association at its general assembly in Venice, May 1961, and is binding on all members of the Association.

A. Personal and Professional Integrity

1. It is understood that by personal integrity is meant the maintenance of both high moral standards and a sound reputation. By professional integrity is meant observance of the Constitution, rules, and, particularly, the Code as adopted by IPRA.

B. Conduct toward Clients and Employers

1. A member has a general duty of fair dealing toward his clients or employers, past and present.

2. A member shall not represent conflicting or competing interests without the express consent of those concerned.

3. A member shall safeguard the confidence of both present and former clients or employers.

4. A member shall not employ methods tending to be derogatory of another member's client or employer.

5. In performing services for a client or employer a member shall not accept fees, commissions, or any other valuable consideration in connection with those services from anyone other than his client or employer without the express consent of his client or employer, given after a full disclosure of the facts.

6. A member shall not propose to a prospective client or employer that his fee or other compensation be contingent on the achievement of certain results; nor shall he enter into any fee agreement to the same effect.

C. Conduct toward the Public and the Media

1. A member shall conduct his professional activities in accordance with the public interest, and with full respect for the dignity of the individual.

2. A member shall not engage in any practice which tends to corrupt the integrity of channels of public communication.

3. A member shall not intentionally disseminate false or misleading information.

4. A member shall at all times seek to give a balanced and faithful representation of the organization which he serves.

5. A member shall not create any organization to serve some announced cause but actually to serve an undisclosed special or private interest of a member or his client or his employer, nor shall he make use of it or any such existing organization.

D. Conduct toward Colleagues

1. A member shall not intentionally injure the professional reputation or practice of another member. However, if a member has evidence

that another member has been guilty of unethical, illegal, or unfair practices in violation of this Code, he should present the information to the Council of IPRA.

2. A member shall not seek to supplant another member with his employer or client.

3. A member shall cooperate with fellow members in upholding and enforcing this Code.

IPR CODE OF PROFESSIONAL CONDUCT

This code defines and implements paragraph 3 (a) (ii) of the Memorandum of the Institute of Public Relations under the heading "Objects," namely "to encourage and foster the observance of high professional standards by its members and to establish and prescribe such standards." Public relations is concerned with the effect of conduct on reputation. The following principles have been laid down to embody this concept and enhance relations between the institute's members and the public to whom they are directly or indirectly responsible in the performance of their duties.

1. *Standards of Professional Conduct.* A member, in the conduct of his professional activities, shall respect the public interest and the dignity of the individual. It is his personal responsibility at all times to deal fairly and honestly with his client or employer, past or present; with his fellow members; with the media of communication; and with the public.

2. *Dissemination of Information.* A member shall not knowingly or recklessly disseminate false or misleading information, and shall use proper care to avoid doing so inadvertently. He has a positive duty to maintain integrity and accuracy.

3. *Media of Communication.* A member shall not engage in any practice that tends to corrupt the integrity of the media of communication.

4. *Undisclosed Interests.* A member shall not be a party to any activity that deliberately seeks to dissemble or mislead by promoting a disguised or undisclosed interest while appearing to further another. It is his duty to ensure that the actual interest of any organization with which he may be professionally concerned is adequately declared.

5. *Confidential Information.* A member shall not disclose (except upon the order of a court of competent jurisdiction) or make use of

information given or obtained in confidence from his employer or client, past or present, for personal gain or otherwise, without express consent.

6. *Conflict of Interests.* A member shall not represent conflicting or competing interests without the express consent of the parties concerned after full disclosure of the facts.

7. *Sources of Payments.* A member, in the course of his professional services to his employer or client, shall not accept payment either in cash or kind in connection with those services from any other source without the express consent of his employer or client.

8. *Disclosure of Financial Interests.* A member having a financial interest in an organization shall not recommend the use of that organization, nor make use of its services on behalf of his client or employer, without declaring his interest.

9. *Payment Contingent upon Achievements.* A member shall not negotiate or agree terms with a prospective employer or client on the basis of payment contingent upon specific future public relations achievements.

10. *Supplanting another Member.* A member seeking employment or new business by direct and individual approach to a potential employer or client shall take all reasonable steps to ascertain whether that employment or business is already carried out by another member. If so, it shall be his duty to advise the other member in advance of any approach he proposes to make to the employer or client concerned. (Nothing in this clause shall be taken as inhibiting a member from the general advertisement of his services.)

11. *Rewards to Holders of Public Office.* A member shall not, with intent to further his interest (or those of his client or employer), offer or give any reward to a person holding public office if such action is inconsistent with the public interest.

12. *Employment of Members of Parliament.* A member who employs a member of Parliament, of either house, in connection with parliamentary matters, whether in a consultative or executive capacity, shall disclose this fact, and also the object of the employment to the general secretary of the institute, who shall enter it in a register kept for the purpose. A member of the institute who is himself a member of Parliament shall be directly responsible for disclosing or causing to be disclosed to the general secretary any such information as may relate to himself. (The register referred to in this clause shall be open to public inspection at the offices of the institute during office hours.)

13. *Injury to other Members.* A member shall not maliciously injure the professional reputation or practice of another member.

14. *Instruction of Others.* A member who knowingly causes or permits another person or organization to act in a manner inconsistent with this code or is party to such action shall himself be deemed to be in breach of it.

15. *Reputation of the Profession.* A member shall not conduct himself in any manner detrimental to the reputation of the Institute or the profession of public relations.

16. *Upholding the Code.* A member shall uphold this code, shall cooperate with fellow members in so doing and in enforcing decisions on any matter arising from its application. If a member has reason to believe that another member has been engaged in practices that may be in breach of this code, it shall be his duty to inform the institute. It is the duty of all members to assist the institute to implement this code, and the institute will support any member so doing.

17. *Other Professions.* A member shall, when acting for a client or employer who belongs to a profession, respect the code of ethics of that other profession and shall not knowingly be party to any breach of such a code.

IPRA AND CERP CODE OF ETHICS

This was adopted by IPRA and CERP in Athens, May 1965, and modified at Tehran in April 1968. It is known as the Code of Athens.

CONSIDERING that all Member countries of the United Nations Organization have agreed to abide by its Charter which reaffirms "its faith in fundamental human rights, in the dignity and worth of the human person" and that having regard to the very nature of their profession, Public Relations practitioners in these countries should undertake to ascertain and observe the principles set out in this Charter;

CONSIDERING that, apart from "rights," human beings have not only physical or material needs but also intellectual, moral, and social needs, and that their rights are of real benefit to them only insofar as these needs are essentially met;

CONSIDERING that, in the course of their professional duties and depending on how these duties are performed, Public Relations practitioners can substantially help to meet these intellectual, moral, and social needs;

And lastly, CONSIDERING that the use of techniques enabling them to come simultaneously into contact with millions of people gives Public Relations practitioners a power that has to be restrained by the observance of a strict moral code.

On all of these grounds, the undersigned Public Relations Associations hereby declare that they accept as their moral charter the principles of the following Code of Ethics, and that if, in the light of evidence submitted to the Council, a member of these associations should be found to have infringed this Code in the course of his professional duties, he will be deemed to be guilty of serious misconduct calling for an appropriate penalty.

Accordingly, each Member of these Associations:

SHALL ENDEAVOR

1. To contribute to the achievement of the moral and cultural conditions enabling human beings to reach their full stature and enjoy the indefeasible rights to which they are entitled under the "Universal Declaration of Human Rights";

2. To establish communication patterns and channels which, by fostering the free flow of essential information, will make each member of the society in which he lives feel that he is being kept informed, and also give him an awareness of his own personal involvement and responsibility, and of his solidarity with other members;

3. To bear in mind that, because of the relationship between his profession and the public, his conduct—even in private—will have an impact on the way in which the profession as a whole is appraised;

4. To respect, in the course of his professional duties, the moral principles and rules of the "Universal Declaration of Human Rights";

5. To pay due regard to, and uphold, human dignity, and to recognize the right of each individual to judge for himself;

6. To encourage the moral, psychological, and intellectual conditions for dialogue in its true sense, and to recognize the right of the parties involved to state their case and express their views,

SHALL UNDERTAKE

7. To conduct himself always and in all circumstances in such a manner as to deserve and secure the confidence of those with whom he comes into contact;

8. To act, in all circumstances, in such a manner as to take account of the respective interests of the parties involved: both the interests of the organization which he serves and the interests of the publics concerned;

9. To carry out his duties with integrity, avoiding language likely to

lead to ambiguity or misunderstanding, and to maintain loyalty to his clients or employers, whether past or present;

SHALL REFRAIN FROM

10. Subordinating the truth to other requirements;

11. Circulating information that is not based on established and ascertainable facts;

12. Taking part in any venture or undertaking that is unethical or dishonest or capable of impairing human dignity and integrity;

13. Using any "manipulative" methods or techniques designed to create subconscious motivations which the individual cannot control of his own free will and so cannot be held accountable for the action taken on them.

Appendix B:

Public Relations Organizations

In this appendix the work of five organizations is considered; these are the Public Relations Society of America, the Institute of Public Relations, the Public Relations Consultants Association, the International Public Relations Association, and the European Public Relations Confederation (CERP).

PUBLIC RELATIONS SOCIETY OF AMERICA

Objectives

The Public Relations Society of America (PRSA) is the major professional association for public relations practitioners and, with a national membership of more than ten thousand persons, it is the largest association of its kind in the world. Chartered in 1947, the society's primary objectives are to advance the standards of the public relations profession and to provide the means for member self-improvement through a series of continuing educational activities, information exchange programs, and research projects, conducted on a national, as well as local, level.

PRSA, as detailed in its articles of incorporation, was formed for the following purposes:

- To unite those engaged in the profession of public relations.
- To consider all matters affecting the practice of public relations.
- To formulate, promote, and interpret to business, professional, and

other groups, and to the general public, the objectives, potentialities, and functions of public relations and those who practice it.

• To improve the relations of public relations workers with employers and clients, with established media on information and opinion, and with the general public.

• To promote and seek to maintain high standards of public service and conduct.

• To exchange ideas and experience, and to collect and disseminate information of value to public relations workers and the public.

• To promote, sponsor, and foster the study of research and instruction in the general field of public relations through lectures and other courses at duly and regularly established institutions of learning.

• To provide facilities and opportunities for research and analysis of any and all features of the public relations field through forums, discussions, surveys, public meetings, exhibitions, and conferences.

• To publish pamphlets, books, monographs, and in general to disseminate information concerning the subject of public relations.

• To give, grant, and sponsor the granting of fellowships and awards in duly recognized institutions of learning for study and research in the field of public relations.

Professional Standards

Acceptance into PRSA requires that individual members adhere to the principles of the Society's Code of Professional Standards for the Practice of Public Relations. In abiding by this code, each PRSA member fulfills his individual responsibility to make the public relations profession worthy of public confidence. Enforcement of the code is monitored by the society's grievance board.

Accreditation Program. In 1965 the society established a program whereby members with at least five years of professional public relations experience may earn PRSA accredited (APR) status by passing written and oral examinations which test their competence in and knowledge of the public relations field. The written examination is supervised by a professional testing organization, and the oral examination conducted by a team of three accredited members. Since 1969 accreditation has been an eligibility requirement for all those who apply for active membership.

Education and Research. The society's various services and activities are designed to help members develop their knowledge and competence at all levels throughout their public relations careers, beginning with the Public Relations Student Society of America (PRSSA) for college undergraduates and continuing through a progression of workshops, seminars, and institutes for more experienced public relations executives.

PRSA educational activities are guided nationally by its committee on education, with the advice of educators from colleges and universities throughout the country. PRSA is an affiliate members of the Association for Education in Journalism and of the American Council on Education for Journalism. The society participates in the ACEJ's program for accrediting public relations courses offered at schools of journalism. A variety of special research projects, in which members participate, are also sponsored by the society, its committees, sections, and the Foundation for Public Relations Research and Education, Inc., and the study results are made available to members.

Professional Development. This is the society's major service to its members at all levels of experience. An integrated program, geared to the career levels of practitioners, offers educational opportunities in many forms and is designed to help members develop their knowledge and maintain their competence in these rapidly changing times. An important element is a self-study program designed to help the individual member improve the skills and knowledge necessary for development and growth as a public relations professional at all levels of practice, from beginner to senior manager. The program involves publications, audio-visual aids, and educational seminars. A national committee on professional development heads the self-study effort.

Public Relations Institute.   Each year, PRSA sponsors a four-day, graduate-level institute, held on the campus of a major university. The institute, devoted to in-depth study and analysis of current problems affecting public relations executives, features outstanding speakers and discussion leaders drawn from education, business, government, communications, and other fields.

Foundation for Public Relations Research and Education, Inc.   The foundation was established in 1956 by members of the Public Relations Society of America to encourage and undertake important research and educational projects in the field of public relations, to grant fellowship awards annually to a selected number of public relations teachers, and to present a graduate scholarship each year to an outstanding public relations student. Other programs conducted by the foundation include an audiovisual archive of important public relations lecturers, case histories, and filmed interviews; a series of monographs dealing with the historical antecedents of the profession; and publication of research data on public relations, including the hard-cover publications *Public Relations Law* and *Public Relations: A Comprehensive Bibliography.* In 1972 the foundation produced *Opinion of the Publics,* the first major motion picture on the public relations profession.

Organization Structure

Membership. There are four categories of membership within the PRSA: accredited, active, associate, and pre-associate. Each category has specific requirements for membership eligibility. PRSA members are employed by business, industrial, and counseling firms; trade and professional associations; educational institutions; health and welfare agencies; government, including the military; and various other organizations.

Chapters, Districts, Assembly. The society is composed of eighty-two chapters grouped in nine geographical districts. Each chapter has its own officers and board of directors, and chapter representatives within each district elect a district chairman who serves as liaison with the chapters, PRSA board of directors and the national headquarters. Each chapter has proportional representation on the society's governing body, the assembly of delegates. National officers and board of directors, as well as district chairmen and section chairmen, are also members of the assembly.

Board of Directors. The board of directors manages and controls the business affairs of the society. It is composed of the society's national officers (president, president-elect, secretary, and treasurer), six directors-at-large, and immediate past president ex officio.

Committees. PRSA committees and task forces, appointed by the board of directors, provide guidance and direction at the policymaking and operational levels of the society in all phases of its activities.

Sections. Within PRSA are ten professional interest sections that provide additional opportunities for members to participate in discussions and exchange views in these specialized areas of public relations practice: association, corporate, counselors, educational institutions, educators, financial institutions, government, health, investor relations, and utilities.

Judicial Panels and Grievance Board. The society's judicial structure consists of six member panels in each of nine districts throughout the United States. The panels are charged with investigating and hearing complaints relating to violations of the society's code, and making recommendations to the board with respect to warning, admonishment, reprimand, censure, suspension, or expulsion of any member found in violation of the code. Complaints may be filed by members or nonmembers with the society's nine-member grievance board. (See PRSA Bylaws, Article XIII).

Membership Services and Activities

The society's headquarters office is in New York City. The staff implements the board's policies and programs, and provides assistance to chapters, districts, committees, sections, and other PRSA groups. The following activities are coordinated by the national staff:

National Conference. The annual conference, the major public relations event each year, brings together representatives of the profession and related fields for study and discussion of subjects important to their growth and development.

Honors and Awards. The society recognizes its members' excellence in public relations with the following annual awards, presented at the National Conference:

> *Gold Anvil Award* for distinguished service to the profession by an individual.
> *Outstanding Educator Award* for performance by a public relations teacher.
> *Paul Lund Award* for outstanding public service.
> *Presidential Citations* for outstanding service to the society.
> *Film Festival Awards* for the best public relations films of the year. (Open to members only.)

Outstanding chapter activities in furthering the public relations profession, as well as PRSA, are recognized by the presentation of *Chapter Banner Awards* at the society's annual Spring National Assembly.

Silver Anvil Awards Competition. PRSA each year conducts the Silver Anvil Awards competition for outstanding public relations programs carried on during the preceding year. Deadline for entries is mid-March each year. The competition is open to members and nonmembers.

Research Information Center. In 1955 the society established the first and only national information center for the field of public relations, designed to meet the study and reference needs of public relations executives, teachers, and students.

The center, located at PRSA national headquarters, collects data on public relations and answers individual requests for information on all phases of the profession. An extensive library of books on public relations and related subjects is housed at the center, where reading and study facilities are provided for visitors. Available to members and nonmembers.

202

Referral Service. As a help to prospective employers seeking public relations talent and to public relations practitioners seeking new positions, the society maintains a referral service at its national headquarters. Several chapters have similar services at local and regional levels. (Available to members only.)

Publications. *Public Relations Journal* is the monthly professional magazine of the society, with subjects ranging from theoretical to practical treatment of topics vital to the profession. *PRSA National Newsletter,* also published monthly, contains news about the society and its members.

The Register issue of the *Journal* is an annual publication which lists all members of the society, their addresses and business affiliations. The Register also contains a directory of current national, district, and chapter officers, committee and task force members, section officers, and other vital data on PRSA groups.

It also carries the PRSA code of professional standards and procedures for judicial panels, certain policies of the board, and the PRSA bylaws.

Channels is a monthly newsletter for nonprofit organizations and agencies and is the oldest continuous publication on public relations, founded in 1937. It is available by subscription.

Government Liaison. The society maintains liaison with public information officers in a variety of federal, state, and local government departments and agencies to provide governmental and legislative information for PRSA members.

Insurance. In 1974 PRSA introduced a program of insurance plans for members. This includes a low-cost, high-indemnity accident insurance program and a group life insurance plan, both administered by Association Insurers Agency, Inc., PH8 Hampton House, 204 E. Joppa Rd., Towson, Md. 21204, 301-296-1031.

The program is in addition to plans for counselors which the counselors section has been offering for some years, including errors and omissions coverage and disability.

International Affiliation. The society is a member of the Inter-American Federation of Public Relations Association (FIARP) and the International Accreditation Council (IAC). A number of PRSA members hold individual membership in the International Public Relations Association (IPRA) and other international public relations groups and national societies.

THE INSTITUTE OF PUBLIC RELATIONS

This is the only organization in the United Kingdom devoted exclusively to the study and development of public relations. It was founded in 1948 by a group of public relations officers from commerce, industry, central and local government, all of whom felt the need for an organization to represent the rapidly expanding profession in which they were engaged. It was incorporated in January 1964.

The institute's main objects are—

(a) to promote the development of public relations for the benefit of the practice in commerce; industry; central and local government; nationalized undertakings; professional, trade, and voluntary organizations and for the benefit of all practitioners, and others concerned in or with public relations.

(b) to encourage and foster the observance of high professional standards by its members and to establish and prescribe such standards.

(c) to arrange meetings, discussions, conferences, etc., on matters of common interest, and generally to act as a clearing house for the exchange of ideas on the practice of public relations.

The constitution of the institute provides for honorary life members, fellows, members, associates, overseas associates, affiliates, student members, and retired members. Honorary life membership and fellowship may be conferred by the council in recognition of outstanding services or of distinguished public relations work. Admission to each remaining category of membership is subject to election by the council, which is advised by the membership committee. Each application is considered carefully on its merits in order to safeguard the professional standards of the institute.

Honorary Life members are individuals, from within or outside the institute, on whom the council is empowered to confer this honor in recognition of outstanding services.

Fellows are members on whom the council has, by secret ballot, conferred fellowships "in recognition of distinguished public relations work." Fellows are entitled to use the suffix FIPR.

Members. Membership of the institute is open to—

(a) individuals who at the date of their application are twenty-eight years of age or more and whose applications are acceptable to the council, providing that they have had at least five years' comprehensive experience in, and that they are qualified to undertake the practice of, public relations as defined in the Memorandum of Association.

(b) individuals who at the date of the application are twenty-six years of age or more and whose applications are acceptable to the council, providing that they have had at least two years' comprehensive experience in, and that they are qualified to undertake the practice of, public relations as defined in the Memorandum of Association; and providing further that they shall have previously been awarded the CAM Diploma in Public Relations or (prior to 1972) that they shall have passed the Institute's Final Examination.

Members are entitled to a membership certificate, to exercise full voting rights in the affairs of the institute, and are also entitled to use the letters, MIPR.

Associates. Associate membership is open to individuals normally resident in the United Kingdom who at the date of their application are twenty-one years of age or more and whose applications are accepted by the council, provided that either

(a) at the time of their application they have been professionally engaged in public relations practice for a minimum period of three years, *or*

(b) at the time of their application they have been so engaged for a minimum period of two years and shall have passed the CAM certificate in public relations or (prior to 1972) the institute's intermediate examination.

Such persons are entitled to use the description Associate of the Institute of Public Relations, and to exercise full voting rights in the affairs of the institute.

Retired Membership. This is open to any fellows, members, or associates who have retired from active business life and whose applications are acceptable to the council.

Overseas Associates. Overseas associate membership is open to individuals normally resident outside the United Kingdom who would qualify for associate membership were they living within the United Kingdom, and whose applications are acceptable to the council.

Affiliates are persons, normally resident in the United Kingdom, who are engaged in public relations work but are not yet eligible for associate membership, or who are associated with or interested in the practice of public relations.

Student Membership. This is open to individuals who at the time of application are taking or proposing to take a course of education or training organized or recognized by the council, and whose applications are acceptable to the council. (For details of these courses see Appendix I.)

The activities of the institute are aimed toward the attainment of its objects—they are educational and social, or a combination of both. One of its most valuable functions is to provide opportunities for the exchange of information and active cooperation among its members.

In addition to the college courses, the institute arranges evening lecturers, discussion meetings, debates, film shows, one-day and weekend conferences—all designed to increase members' knowledge of the theory and practice of public relations.

Monthly luncheon meetings are held in London from September until June, to which are invited distinguished guest speakers from industry, government, the professions, and so on.

The institute publishes a monthly newsletter, *Public Relations*— the only publication of its kind in this country devoted solely to the subject. In addition, the institute publishes many reports and monographs on specific aspects of public relations practice.

The institute's constitution provides for both vocational and regional groups. At present, there is a group for members who are local government public relations officers, and there are eight regional groups, which arrange their own meetings and other events, in the East Midlands, West Midlands, Northeast, Northwest, West of England, East Anglia, Scotland, South Wales, Wessex, and Northern Ireland.

Inquiries should be addressed to the Director, Institute of Public Relations, 1 Great James Street, London WC1N 3DA Tel: 01-405 5505).

THE PUBLIC RELATIONS CONSULTANTS ASSOCIATION

The PRCA, unlike other associations, consists of corporate as opposed to individual membership. It is a trade association, formed in November 1969, with the objectives of promoting the growth of public relations consultancy, improving the standards of consultancy practice, providing facilities for various publics to confer with consultants as a body, and promoting confidence in consultancy only. It recommends individual membership of the IPR, with which it cooperates closely.

The association is governed by a board of management elected by the membership. Some of the association's activities include research on behalf of its members and working parties in specialist areas of public relations whose findings are published by the secretariat.

The PRCA has had contact with consultancies in several countries with a view to extending its activities worldwide or to encourage the establishment of national associations similar to the PRCA.

INTERNATIONAL PUBLIC RELATIONS ASSOCIATION

The international idea in the field of public relations was born in 1949, when two Dutch and three British public relations men met in London. They talked about their work in public relations, and of organizing public relations officers in collective groups with the object of raising the standard of public relations practice and enhancing the prestige as well as the efficiency of public relations men.

The next step came in 1950, when a group of public relations officers from France, Great Britain, the Netherlands, Norway, and the United States of America met in Holland and issued a statement that having—

> considered the necessity of furthering the skill and ethics of their profession and of a clearer understanding of their work, and considered **further the value of international exchange of information and cooperation** they had resolved that a provisional International Committee be set up with the object of furthering such exchange and cooperation and the eventual establishment of an International Public Relations Association.

A provisional international committee was formed, and over the next five years held talks in England, mainly in conjunction with the weekend conference of the British Institute of Public Relations. The meetings were attended by representatives from France, Great Britain, the Netherlands, Norway, and the United States, and observers from Australia, Belgium, Canada, Finland, Italy, and Switzerland.

Finally, the International Public Relations Association was brought into being in May 1955 at a meeting at Stratford-upon-Avon, when the constitution was formally adopted, and the first council appointed.

The policy and purpose of the IPRA is to—

(a) Provide a channel for the exchange of ideas and professional experience between those engaged in public relations practice of international significance.

(b) Form a Rotary in which members at any time in need of advice and guidance may be assured of the goodwill and assistance of fellow members throughout the world.

(c) Foster the highest standards of public relations practice generally in all countries and, in particular, in the international field.

(d) Further the practice of public relations in all parts of the world and to enhance its value and influence by the promotion of knowledge and understanding of its objects and methods both inside and outside the profession.

(e) Review and seek solutions to problems affecting public relations practice common to various countries, including such questions as the status of the profession, codes of professional ethics, and qualifications to practice.

(f) Publish bulletins, journals, or other publications, including an *International Who's Who in Public Relations.*

(g) Undertake such other activities as may be deemed likely to benefit members or to contribute to the advancement of public relations practice throughout the world.

Membership is open to persons devoting their full time to and being fully responsible for the planning and execution of a coherent and significant part of the whole of the activities of a corporation, company, union, government, government department, or other organization in establishing and maintaining sound and productive relations with special publics or the public at large so as to adapt itself to its environment and to interpret itself to society, provided that these activities shall possess international significance.

Members are not entitled to use any description, title, or letters other than that of "Member of the International Public Relations Association" to signify their connection with the association.

The IPRA remains a society of individuals and has resisted attempts to turn it into a world federation.

EUROPEAN PUBLIC RELATIONS CONFEDERATION

There have been a number of federations formed in different parts of the world by national public relations associations to provide opportunity for contacts and discussion of mutual problems.

One of the most successful of these federations has been the European Public Relations Confederation (CERP). The membership consists of professional public relations associations of European countries, and in this respect it differs from both the IPR and IPRA, which are composed entirely of individual members.

CERP meets annually and has three main standing committees. The first, the European Conference of National Public Relations Associations (CEDAN), has the purpose of coordinating the activities of the public relations associations and membership in order to reach agreement on professional practice and ethics. The second standing committee, the European Study Group for Public Relations and Communications Techniques (CEDET), studies problems of training, education, and professional development. The third standing committee, the European Committee for the Application and Development of Public Relations (CEDAP), is concerned with the development of public relations practice in Europe.